TEACHING
ENGLISH FOR
Reconciliation

TEACHING ENGLISH FOR
Reconciliation

PURSUING PEACE THROUGH
TRANSFORMED RELATIONSHIPS
IN LANGUAGE LEARNING AND TEACHING

JAN EDWARDS DORMER

CHERYL WOELK

Teaching English for Reconciliation: Pursuing Peace through Transformed Relationships in Language Learning and Teaching
© 2018 by Jan Edwards Dormer and Cheryl Woelk

Published by William Carey Library
1605 E. Elizabeth St.
Pasadena, CA 91104 | www.missionbooks.org

Melissa Hughes, editor
Kathy Curtis, interior design
Yvonne Parks, cover design

William Carey Library is a ministry of
Frontier Ventures
www.frontierventures.org

Printed in the United States of America
22 21 20 19 18   5 4 3 2 1 BP 750

Library of Congress Cataloging-in-Publication Data
Names: Dormer, Jan Edwards, author.
Title: Teaching English for reconciliation : pursuing peace through transformed relationships in language learning and teaching / Jan Edwards Dormer and Cheryl Woelk.
Description: Pasadena : William Carey Library, 2018.
Identifiers: LCCN 2017052896 (print) | LCCN 2017057964 (ebook) | ISBN 9780878088751 (ebook) | ISBN 9780878085439 (print)
Subjects: LCSH: Peace—Study and teaching. | Reconciliation—Study and teaching. | English language—Study and teaching—Social aspects.
Classification: LCC JZ5534 (ebook) | LCC JZ5534.D67 2018 (print) | DDC 303.6/6071—dc23
LC record available at https://lccn.loc.gov/2017052896

DEDICATION

To my students and colleagues, who have helped me learn
about the importance of relationship in the English language
classroom, and to my family, who continue to patiently
listen to and support my passion for ministry and service
through English language teaching.

~Jan

To my students, teachers, colleagues and friends who
have taught me about peace through all your many languages,
and to Hong Soek and Rohan for our practice
of peacebuilding together.

~Cheryl

CONTENTS

Introduction ix

PART 1:
THE FOUNDATION:
WHY TEACH ENGLISH FOR RECONCILIATION?

Ch. 1: Teaching for Conflict Resolution, Peacebuilding, and
Reconciliation.. 2
Ch. 2: Intersections of Language Learning and
Reconciliation.. 17
Ch. 3: A Framework for Christians Teaching English for
Reconciliation.. 27

PART 2:
THE PEOPLE:
WHO IS INVOLVED IN TEACHING ENGLISH
FOR RECONCILIATION?

Ch. 4: Community.. 40
Ch. 5: Learners... 56
Ch. 6: Teachers... 73

PART 3:
THE RESOURCES:
HOW CAN WE TEACH ENGLISH FOR RECONCILIATION?

Ch. 7: Creating Curricula for Peace and Reconciliation.................. 90
Ch. 8: Adapting Curricula for Peace and Reconciliation 119
Ch. 9: Suggestions for Diverse Settings and Goals......................... 135

APPENDICES

Appendix A: Suggested Activities..148
Appendix B: Sample Forms and Plans 162
Appendix C: Resources 176

References...179

FIGURES

1. Three Lenses of a Teaching English within a Reconciliation
   Framework...33
2. Sources and Domains of Power...63
3. REAL Activities in Teaching English for Reconciliation.. 82, 102
4. Reconciliatory English Teaching Framework..................... 93, 122

TABLES

1. Aligning Skill Sets for Reconciliatory Goals 105
2. Integration of Differentiating Factors with the Reconciliatory
   English Teaching Framework..140

About the Authors 183
Additional Resources 185

INTRODUCTION

A STORY FROM THE PAST . . .

A novice English as a Second Language teacher in the early 1990s, I (Jan) nervously walked through the door on the first day of a new class for adult refugees in Canada. I had been told that the majority of the twenty students in this new class would be coming from Eastern Europe. I was aware that there was a war in Yugoslavia, and had heard about fighting between "Serbians" and "Croatians." But that was miles away from my comfortable life in Ontario, where my husband and I had settled into a pastorate and the raising of two young children. I was enjoying finally getting into my profession after completing an MA in TESOL (Teaching English to Speakers of Other Languages). I was excited about this new group of students, and eagerly anticipated seeing them become proficient in English under my expert tutelage.

As I walked through the door on that first day, my thoughts were on the engaging ice-breaker activities I had designed so that we could get to know each other. The English classroom is a very relational space, so I envisioned my students becoming fast friends very quickly. I felt confident in my ability to foster a classroom atmosphere which would have them talking, laughing, and building relationships as they learned the English words and phrases with which they would build a new life in Canada. They would fall in love with English, Canada, and the classroom space in which we would all spend many hours together over the next six months.

But all of these lofty, relational ideals came crashing down within the first ten minutes of class. Upon entering the classroom, I was a little taken aback by the students' worried facial expressions and by the silence in the room. I had taught other groups of students who were just arriving in Canada, and had always found that students would try their best to get to know each other right away. Goodwill had nearly always prevailed, as students reached out to each other with smiles and friendly gestures when a common language was not available, and in animated chatter when they spoke the same language. Usually, students seemed grateful for the government program that provided free English classes for them, and were eager to get to know their classmates and teacher.

Not this group, however. They sat silent, grim, and fearful. Confident in my ability to rally the most reluctant student, I greeted the class with enthusiasm and warmth, and then invited them to share their names and where they were from. I looked to my left, indicating that the first student should begin, and then we would proceed around the circle. Haltingly, soberly, the first student gave his name, followed by the word "Croatia." The next student followed suit, mirroring the first student's reluctance to speak. This was not going well! Then the third student stood up, and motioned for me to follow him to talk outside the classroom.

Uh oh, I thought. What have I done wrong? The man that stood before me seemed to have a higher level of English proficiency than the others, which was perhaps why he had taken charge of the situation. Though his English was sparse and halting, his message was clear: "We don't want to say our names. If we say our country, people won't like us. We are from Serbia and Croatia . . . and we cannot study together."

I was stunned. I had not once considered the possibility that my new class of refugees from the Yugoslav war might bring this war into my classroom. As I look back on the situation now, I am a little reluctant to admit my short-sightedness and my obliviousness to the plight of these students. However, I had had no previous experiences or training which might have alerted me to the possibility of animosity within the English classroom. There was no orientation at my college to prepare me for the issues of identity and conflict that may emerge when teaching English to refugees. I had been born into an American Midwestern farm family, grown up in Brazil after my parents became missionaries there, and then married a

Canadian. War had never come into my life in any way other than the nightly news.

I don't know how I made it through the rest of that first day. The confrontation with the student had so thrown me, that I decided I needed to play it very safe, and just work through a course book in that class. My preference was to use more student-centered activities and minimize the use of textbooks, but I had no idea how to design activities for a group of students who appeared to be defensive and frightened. Something good did come out of that long-ago experience, however, because it alerted me to the potential for conflict within an English language classroom. As God later took my husband and me on an unexpected path which included years of service in Indonesia, Brazil, and Kenya, I had opportunities to engage with other similar groups of learners. I discovered that whether differences stemmed from differing ethnicities, tribal allegiances, religious affiliations, socioeconomic status, or even gender and age, prejudice and animosity can complicate the teaching of English.

But what I have also discovered over the years is that the English learning classroom can be an exciting space in which diverse students can acquire a common language and new skills which can begin to break down barriers between them. English learners can acquire dialogic skills which include not only a new language but also more "other-centered" perspectives. They can learn words and phrases pertaining to topics such as forgiveness, empathy, and peacebuilding, even as they develop language. And the ever-present topic of culture in the language classroom can foster a new appreciation for different worldviews and perspectives. Finally, in many English teaching ministry endeavors there is potential for Christian English teachers to create a space in which learners may be able to experience the fullness of reconciliation— reconciling with others and with their Creator through the movement of God within us and through us.

The Structure of the Book

This book aims to help English language teachers create classroom spaces in which students can engage in this kind of learning. It begins by introducing the *why* of teaching English for reconciliation. This section provides a background in related areas of study such as conflict resolution and peace education, highlights the uniqueness of an English language classroom in its potential to promote new ways of thinking, and finally links these understandings to Scripture, building a solid theological foundation for reconciliatory English teaching on which a Christian English teacher can stand.

The second section of the book addresses *who* should be involved in teaching English for reconciliation. With chapters on the community, the learners and their identities, and finally the teacher, the human element of reconciliation is thoroughly explored. Readers will develop a strong understanding of the various agents in efforts towards conflict resolution, peacebuilding, and other types of reconciliatory endeavors. In the last chapter in this section, readers will focus in on the pivotal role of the teacher and how the teacher's character and methodologies are both critical in teaching English for reconciliation.

In the last section, the framework for reconciliatory English teaching is revisited, this time fleshed out with explanations of how each part of the framework is utilized in real teaching situations. The first chapter is devoted to contexts in which the teacher has freedom to make reconciliation an overt part of the course. The next chapter is written for those working in contexts in which the curriculum is already established, providing readers with suggestions for adapting curricula for peace and reconciliation. In the final chapter, the concepts presented throughout the book are seen through the lens of specific contexts, such as church-based English teaching, teaching refugees, or teaching in international ministry settings.

TERMINOLOGY

Finally, we would like to set the stage for the reader in understanding some of the terms we have chosen to use in this book. The term "reconciliation" is often used to mean a full and complete restoration of a relationship. We understand that it may be unlikely for this kind of reconciliation to be achieved in an English class. Some of the many barriers to actually arriving at true reconciliation in an English class might include the fact that such deep emotional work may be best undertaken in the first language. There may not be sufficient time in an English class, and we have a responsibility to keep the learning of English as the main goal of an English class. So, if we acknowledge that actual reconciliation in an English class may be rare, what is it that we think *can* happen in English classes? It is the *pursuit* of reconciliation. When we teach English *for* reconciliation, we suggest that reconciliation might be an ultimate outcome from some of the experiences in the English class. It was with this thought in mind that we settled on using the adjective *reconciliatory* for a person, activity, idea, or resource which might foster skills or ways of thinking which could be stepping stones toward reconciliation.

Another term used frequently in this book is *peacebuilding.* As both an adjective and an activity, peacebuilding is one of the stepping stones towards reconciliation and represents a field of study made up of theories and practice to strategically work at creating peace between people and in societies. *Conflict resolution* is also used often throughout the book as a set of specific skills which support peacebuilding and could lead to reconciliation.

Finally, we do use a few terms related to the teaching of English. *English as a second/subsequent language (ESL)* is what English learners study and acquire in contexts where English is a dominant language, such as the United States, Canada, Great Britain, and Australia. *English as a Foreign Language (EFL)* is what English learners study in K-12 schools or in specialized English schools, in countries where English is not a dominant language, such as Brazil, Indonesia, and Korea. We have experience teaching in both of these settings, and believe that the ideas in this book are relevant for both.

CONCLUSION

It is our hope that this book will be a thought-provoking yet practical resource for Christians who take seriously the biblical mandate to be involved in the "ministry of reconciliation" (2 Cor 5:18). We also hope that educators who do not identify as Christian will find valuable tools and inspiration to pursue goals of peace-building and reconciliation within their English classrooms.

As readers become aware of the rich potential for *pursuing peace through transformed relationships in English language learning and teaching*, the lives of the students in these classrooms may be forever changed as they leave not only with greater English proficiency, but also with skills that can bring peace and hope to their families and communities.

PART 1

THE FOUNDATION:
WHY TEACH ENGLISH FOR
RECONCILIATION?

CHAPTER 1

TEACHING FOR CONFLICT RESOLUTION, PEACEBUILDING, AND RECONCILIATION

INTRODUCTION

While writing this book, some of our friends and colleagues reacted with puzzled looks upon hearing the title *Teaching English for Reconciliation.* "What do you mean by that, and how do you do it?" was the sometimes unspoken sentiment. In this first part of the text, we attempt to provide the answer to the question of *why* by providing foundational understanding in three areas: the field of peace, reconciliation and conflict, the field of language and language learning, and Scripture.

First, however, let's take a moment to address the meanings of the words in the title of this book. *Teaching English* may be fairly straightforward. The English language is taught and learned all around the world, and is the de facto "lingua franca" today. Our use of this term includes any and all English learning contexts—from school children learning English in Bolivia to immigrants learning English in Canada to business executives learning English in Hong Kong. The teaching contexts could be formal educational institutions, or more informal classes in home or church environments. One term often used for this diverse field is TESOL (Teaching English to Speakers of Other Languages). Everywhere that English is being learned, there is potential for coupling it with reconciliation!

This second term in the title, *reconciliation,* is the trickier term to define. While our understanding of this word will become clearer in each successive chapter, at the outset we define it as the restoration of relationships, particularly where there has been a history of harm, conflict, or misunderstanding. Even when a particular harm has not happened, reconciliation can occur as people engage in beliefs, attitudes, and actions which foster better relationships between individuals or groups. Various terms are used in different fields of research and practice that relate to this idea, including peacebuilding, peace education, and conflict resolution. We have these ideas in mind when we use the word "reconciliation." As Christians, however, peace between people is not our only concern with reconciliation. We also hope that our English students will experience the interrelated reconciliation with their Creator through the work of Jesus Christ, who gives us both the gift and the ministry of reconciliation. This aspect of *teaching English for reconciliation* will also show up in some of the chapters in this book.

HISTORICAL AND THEORETICAL FOUNDATIONS

The emerging fields of peace education and peacebuilding relate closely to teaching English for reconciliation. As others have pointed out, the idea of building peace through education is not a new idea and appears throughout history and in cultures around the world (Burns and Aspeslagh 2014; Keeves and Watanabe 2013). So, peace education did not start out as a comprehensive field, but has emerged from these different cultural and educational contexts, overlapping and intersecting the fields of education and peacebuilding. In some cases, educators are interested and working in peacebuilding, and in others, peacebuilders are working in education. The field of peacebuilding "seeks to prevent, reduce, transform, and help people recover from violence in all forms, even structural violence that has not yet led to massive civil unrest. At the same time, it empowers people to foster relationships at all levels that sustain them and their environment" (Schirch 2004). Educational programs for reconciliation and peacebuilding are varied and may have different goals, approaches, and concepts that include acquiring skills, understanding the causes of violence, changing attitudes, and even healing from trauma (Salomon and

Nevo 2002). Teaching English for reconciliation encompasses the diversity and complexity of these fields as well.

An important value in peace education is empowering learners through creating meaning together and acting that meaning out in the classroom and beyond (Harris and Morrison 2012). This is a focus on building authentic relationships so that learners can work together to create positive change in their lives and communities. In education, this is often described as a constructivist approach which sees learners as actively involved in putting knowledge together and recognizing how the contexts and structures that surround them shape their learning. Paulo Freire's (2000) foundational work relates to this key aspect of participation and empowerment, highlighting the role of education in enabling people to make change within their contexts. In peace education, the educator's role in this process is less like a fountain of knowledge poured out to the students, and more like a facilitator and co-participant working to create a healthier and more peaceful society.

Within the field of English language teaching, integration of peace education and peacebuilding research and practice has started to take place in a variety of ways. In some contexts, English language teachers have used materials from global issues to address meaningful topics for conversation. In others, English language teaching has been shaped by critical education, which has played an important role in considering learner agency and empowerment, as well as larger issues of power and oppression related to language. Some researchers and educational leaders have used terms such as social justice or social responsibility to speak broadly of issues of language in relation to various forms of violence, oppression, and conflict. English language teachers have also been influenced by diversity education and multicultural education literature and training. The book *Social Justice in English Language Teaching* (Hastings and Jacob 2016) published by TESOL International Association demonstrates just how influential peace-related research and practice has become for English language teachers.

Given the broad nature of the historical and theoretical foundations of teaching for peacebuilding, peace education, and social justice, there's much that can be applied to our goal of teaching English for reconciliation. But where do we start? The rest of this chapter will introduce five conceptual approaches to teaching English for reconciliation that are drawn from the fields of language learning and peacebuilding: relationships, issues, skills, methodologies, and systems.

APPROACHES TO TEACHING ENGLISH FOR RECONCILIATION

These conceptual approaches to teaching English for reconciliation are summaries of what appear throughout the diverse fields of peace education and peacebuilding in relation to English language teaching. They are some of the main ways that peace practitioners and researchers envision building peace through education, and they relate directly to our discussion of the English language classroom. Each section begins with a description of the approach to provide some background and ideas for further reading, followed by ways the approach applies to English language teaching.

RELATIONSHIPS

The first approach that often emerges when educators notice the need for peace is a focus on people connecting face-to-face. The relationship approach suggests that reconciliation happens when people from across conflict lines meet in person and get to know each other as human beings. Based on Allport's (1954) contact hypothesis, this does not mean that just by getting together people will solve their conflicts, but that under certain conditions, individuals from groups in conflict meeting face-to-face can help these groups move towards reconciliation. These conditions include a supportive and cooperative environment, equal status between members of conflicting groups, close enough contact, and a certain amount of motivation to overcome differences (Tal-Or, Boninger, and Gleicher 2002). Many projects use this as their underlying approach to creating a context for reconciliation. One example is a youth peace program in Israel and Palestine called the NIR School of the Heart, which brings together a high school from each cultural group for intensive science courses using English as a common language. Another is the cultural exchanges, run by Mennonite Central Committee, which invite young people to spend a year in another country, living with a host family and volunteering at a local organization. The hope is that these quality encounters will help to transform individuals' beliefs, attitudes, and behaviors towards the other.

For English teachers, this approach may provide an opportunity for reconciliation when we have multiple cultures in one class. Even if students are not necessarily coming from countries or regions in conflict, emphasizing good relationships can be a helpful way to encourage reconciliation across very different worldviews. For example, one of my (Cheryl's) classes had several students each from Saudi Arabia and from the Dominican Republic. At the beginning, there were quite a few judgmental comments from one group to the other and an argument regarding one of our discussion topics cropped up in class. Each group had very different viewpoints and there were a few vocal people on each side who made it known what they considered culturally acceptable or not. After the argument, I was more careful about the topics we brought up and tended to avoid ones that I knew would cause further difficulty. Instead, I focused on creating a sense of community in the classroom, using lots of activities in small groups and partners where they got to know one another on "safe" topics, and doing a few fun activities like participating in a field trip. Over the course of these activities, students gradually warmed to one another. During the break time, I even saw two girls, one from the Dominican Republic and one from Saudi Arabia, joking and laughing while watching a video, then walk away with arms linked. Toward the end of the semester, our textbook brought up another difficult topic. This time, however, there was a much more nuanced discussion. The strong relationships we had built in the class prompted students to use less dogmatic language like, "In my opinion," and hedging, such as "could be" or "might be," in their speaking. They were more willing to listen and by the end, came to the conclusion that different cultures could have very different perspectives, but there was no argument.

A focus on building good relationships can be very effective in working for reconciliation and peace. Meeting face-to-face in many cases is a prerequisite for any kind of peacebuilding dialogue. Since many educators know intuitively what makes for a healthy community, this is also a fairly simple approach. Paul Born (2014) describes sharing stories, having fun together, helping each other, and working together on a common goal as key elements of building community, all of which are quite easy to facilitate in a language learning class and align well with language-learning goals. However, this approach on its own does not necessarily lead to reconciliation. Once the relationships with the immediate group become more distant, the learning can be forgotten. Also, if there is contact between two conflicting groups only through a narrow network, such as children in an English class connecting across divisions without their parents, conflict can actually get worse. For example, parents may continue the fighting even though their children may be learning to get along in class. This puts a great deal of pressure on the children and can even cause more problems in the community. Working at broadening the contact group, in this case including parents, and integrating some of the following approaches in addition to relationship-building can alleviate these concerns.

ISSUES

A second approach to education for peace and reconciliation is a focus on issues. The underlying assumption here is that reconciliation happens when people learn about the issues that divide people and increase their awareness of peacebuilding, or in other words, that knowledge leads to changed behaviour. There are many educational resources under the themes of peace education, global issues, global citizenship, citizenship education, and other terms. UNESCO has a number of resources aimed at creating a "Culture of Peace" and the Asia-Pacific Centre of Education for International Understanding (APCEIU) has developed a number of curricula which are used around the world to shape classroom discussions and decisions about issues. This is an easy way to integrate peace and reconciliation into education because pretty much any topic can be viewed and discussed through a reconciliatory lens.

There is also a lot of support for English teachers who want to address issues from a peace and reconciliation perspective. TESOL International Association has specific interest sections that members can join, such as social responsibility, intercultural communication, and refugee support, which all connect with peace-related themes and provide resources for discussion of issues from a reconciliation perspective. Most contemporary textbooks contain global issues topics and some textbooks are dedicated to critical thinking or specific peace-related issues. One adult English language learning class in Canada that I (Cheryl) observed had a unit related to environmental security, talking about the need to care for the environment in order to promote global peace: in other words, a reconciliation with and through nature. This particular class learned about recycling in their communities and decided to make a class project of monitoring changes they could make in their class, homes, and places of work to reduce consumption and recycle more. Another example of using issues for promoting reconciliation is a Northeast Asia Youth Peace Camp at which youth learn about the history of other countries in their region through English. Hearing these different stories from another perspective and asking questions of participants from those countries helped them to change their perception of the "other."

A focus on issues is easily integrated into existing curricula because sometimes all it takes are thoughtful questions to promote reflection on the topics at hand. While this approach is commonly used for its advantages of awareness building, promoting advocacy, and increasing knowledge of peace and reconciliation, one weakness is that it is hard to make the transition from knowledge to behavior. In fact, recent work actually suggests that behavior comes first when lasting positive change happens. Additionally, in many English teaching contexts around the world, explicit talk of peace or reconciliation is not appropriate. A final weakness of this approach is that it is tempting to move into the "hero/victim dichotomy," which is the tendency to divide people into the heroes who save the victims from their suffering and victims who have little power to change their situation (Lakey 2010). Teachers can start to take on the hero identity, or it might be that students take on that identity to try to save others in their community or around the world. In reality, everyone has power to make change in their contexts to some extent, and supporting people to make change is much more nuanced than coming in as a peace hero.

SKILLS

Another theory of how change happens in education suggests that people reconcile when we change our behaviours and build habits of acting and communicating in peaceful ways. This is the focus of skill-building training programs and experiential learning approaches. Conflict resolution education, peer mediation, non-violent communication, intercultural communication, and culturally sensitive or diversity training all attempt to move from talking about reconciliation and peace to practicing it in class, with the idea that these skills will extend beyond the classroom borders.

In English language teaching, skill-building approaches are already a strength in learning language skills. So, it is relatively easy to connect to skills related to peace, conflict, and reconciliation as many of these are also communication skills. The fields of peace linguistics, which looks at how language can be used to promote peace, and peace sociolinguistics, which looks at how language contributes to peace processes in society, have emerged from language educators who recognize the connection between language skills and conflict resolution. The TESOL International Association "Intercultural Communication" interest section posits that language needs to be focused on skills for communication between cultures, and there is a growing amount of research on intercultural competence in teacher education. In Korea, I (Cheryl) worked with an English class called "Peacebuilders" made up of adult learners interested in improving their communication skills for conflict resolution. Throughout the course, they began to use skills such as active listening, paraphrasing, checking understanding, and nonviolent communication in their inter- actions with each other. They also talked about how these skills were seeping into their interactions in Korean, as well as when they spoke in English!

Another class I taught in Canada had a unit focused on listening skills for healthy communication. As part of the practice, we did individual opinion surveys on controversial topics and then inter- viewed each other, focusing on using the active listening skills to hear differing opinions without judgment. I wasn't sure how this exercise would go as we had several opinionated participants who frequently moved into debate mode with each other even on simple issues! As I monitored and reminded people of the goal of the exer- cise, prompting them to move back to active listening whenever debate-style responses emerged, I started to hear it working. In our debrief afterward, participants shared their experience. They said it "felt different" than when they usually talked about these types of topics. One participant who had frequently jumped into debate mode in the past, admitted that he had been skeptical of the exercise, but in the end enjoyed it. He said it had allowed him to hear what he normally wouldn't have heard and to build under- standing with his conversation partner.

Skills-focused approaches to teaching English for reconciliation can be very practical, empowering learners for daily interactions that they can implement immediately. Participants in skills-fo- cused courses often comment that they feel they have gotten "tools" to use in their lives when seeking conflict resolution or reconciliation. One downside to this approach, however, is that it is usually individually based, focusing on interpersonal conflict and reconciliation, while leaving out larger systemic, cultural, or struc- tural aspects of reconciliation. Skills training for teachers of skills- based classes is extremely important as modeling is an essential part of this approach. Skills approaches can also be problematic when only some members of community are trained, such as in a class that teaches women to use these skills with their husbands. Their spouses may not recognize the value of the skills or may even resist a change in communication patterns. Having spouses learn together, or at least providing an opportunity for husbands to join the class from time to time, would increase the effectiveness of these classes. A multi-faceted approach to skills training that involves students, teachers, administrators, parents, and community members is much more effective.

METHODOLOGIES

Another focus of teaching English for reconciliation can be a methodological approach. The understanding here is that reconciliation happens when we create space for reconciliation within our learning communities. The idea is that how we teach is just as important, if not more important, than what we teach. This approach frequently draws on the works of Paulo Freire (2000) and others and involves participatory education, direct education, experiential learning, teamwork, attention to group dynamics, power studies, and trauma-sensitive teaching. The specific method may vary depending on the group that a teacher is working with, but the idea is that methodologies matter and require our intention and attention.

Methodology is also a key topic in English language teaching, and teachers can add a "reconciliatory lens" as they choose methods. For English teachers, learner-centered teaching, communicative language teaching, task-based language teaching, and other methods (see further details on methodologies in chapter 6) tend to align well with the more participatory and experiential approaches that put the experience and voice of the participants at the center of the learning experience. It's tempting to think that using this approach will directly cause some kind of reconciliation. But reconciliation does not work in a linear, cause-and-effect manner. Instead, teachers can set up the space for reconciliation to potentially happen, and they can intervene when this space is not there.

My (Cheryl's) realization about the importance of participatory methods came from an academic research and writing class in which I assigned a group project that lasted over the course of the semester. At the beginning of the term, I provided a brief overview of the concepts of group process, looking at different roles of people in groups and how that shapes group dynamics. I thought this would give students an idea of how to respond when they had problems in their groups. Despite my efforts, one group struggled when two members repeatedly found themselves in open arguments, and they soon refused to speak to each other. As a result, their group work was not progressing and they ended up missing their final presentation. From this experience, I learned to integrate experiential team-building and communication tasks into group projects, emphasizing learning through participatory methods rather than just giving a handout about group process.

Being intentional about methodologies that allow space for reconciliation and peacebuilding recognizes the classroom as a group, not just a collection of individuals, and promotes an awareness and learning of group dynamics—a key tool for building peace in other contexts as well. The challenge to this approach is that there is heavy reliance on the teacher to set up the space, requiring knowledge of diverse methodologies and the ability to facilitate them. Also, it can be tempting to assume that the buzz of participation and team interaction means that good interaction is taking place, even though this may not be the case. If the teacher does not take the time to create a safe enough space prior to initiating student participation, the resulting interaction could actually cause more harm than good by reinforcing power imbalances or pulling up deeper issues that cannot be dealt with in the class setting, such as responses to trauma. We need to be aware of the results of our methods and watch closely for the impact they have on our learners.

SYSTEMS

Finally, educators teaching English for reconciliation can use system tools as an approach. The theory behind this is that reconciliation happens when a community works together to discern what reconciliation looks like in its specific context and pursues it. This means that each community needs to discern the meaning of reconciliation in its context. Narrative theory, which inspired the growing fields of narrative negotiation and mediation, helps us see how our worldviews and narratives shape our spaces, conflicts, and communities. This approach in education looks at the whole educational institution and social context in addition to what is going on in the classroom or at the interpersonal level. For example, peace education programs held in places of active violent conflict will look significantly different than those in relatively stable societies (Salomon 2002). Restorative justice approaches in education are systems-based approaches which recognize that how we deal with disturbances in the classroom and school have everything to do with how students learn. In Australian public schools, multicultural education from a systems-based perspective seeks reconciliation among cultural groups by including all voices in all aspects of decision-making in the system. Whole-school approaches like Castro's work in the Philippines look at how every aspect of the school is aligned with values of peace and reconciliation (Navarro-Castro and Nario-Galace 2010). Tools such as sustained dialogue can help to work at systemic issues from within an educational institution (Saunders 2012).

For English teachers, this might be the most challenging approach to teaching English for reconciliation, as it involves more than just an isolated teacher in an isolated classroom. It involves collaboration with colleagues, administrators, and students. However, it can start as simply as creating integrated learning options for English language learners in universities, rather than isolating them from other students on campus while they are building their English proficiency skills. It can mean having learners involved in decision-making for classroom or department policies. It can also mean paying attention to institutional realities and how they influence learning, such as where the intensive English program is located on campus, how teachers are separated from each other, administration, or students in their workspace, or whether announcements are received by international students in ways they can access.

Recognizing the larger social contexts—including the varied dynamics of English as a Foreign Language (EFL) versus English as a second/subsequent language (ESL), the social, political, and economic power of English, colonial legacies, linguistic rights realities, and other uncomfortable issues—can bring us to a place where we wonder whether it's even okay to teach English at all! But if we sit with these questions and talk about them together, we may also discover ways to transform our systems into more peaceful places where learners are empowered and valued.

One experience of working with a systems-based approach occurred when I (Cheryl) was administrating a program that used mediation and two Iraqi refugees, who had been on opposing sides of the conflict back home, ended up in the same English class in Canada. From the very first class, they struggled to get along, resulting in heated arguments and even tears. After a couple of these incidents, the teacher came to me exhausted and overwhelmed. We decided to talk to each of the students to hear their perspectives and find out if they would be willing to try mediation. The students agreed, but asked that parents, other staff who spoke their languages, and the teacher be involved. We had a series of meetings and finally came to a consensus on strategies for the two students to continue learning in the same class and a plan to monitor the situation. Knowing the larger context and involving families to support the students helped us to have realistic expectations of their interactions and create a safer classroom for both students.

The systems-based approach looks to long-term community-wide transformation: reconciliation on a social level. However, this approach could be risky. It may change the shape of our work, and we may not know where it will lead. There are no clear guidelines or textbooks for these paths! It's easy to feel like we are getting lost and to get discouraged. Teachers, students, and communities need to work together both for change to happen and to encourage one another on the way.

Practical Application: Building on Historical and Theoretical Foundations

1. *Use a variety of approaches to connect with peace and reconciliation in the classroom.* Consider your teaching context and experiment with these five approaches in your lesson plans (See chapter 7 for more on lesson planning.). Find what your learners get excited about and where their interests lie in relation to reconciliation work.

2. *Learn about the foundations of peace education and teaching for reconciliation in your contexts.* Education for peace and reconciliation is not new or unique to English-speaking cultures. Ask questions about educational approaches and school programs that your students know about. Learn about historical movements for peace in the community and how education may have played a part. Develop a contact list of names of people from the community who are involved in reconciliation work and reach out to them to learn and collaborate.

3. *Recognize that reconciliation can look very different in every situation.* Avoid the temptation to envision a reconciliatory outcome for someone else. Instead, engage them in envisioning a more peaceful relationship together. Be open to ways that reconciliation may turn out differently than you expected. Affirm even small steps towards peace while acknowledging there is more work to be done.

4. *Talk about teaching English for reconciliation.* Share openly about your ideas for the English classroom with students and colleagues as much as possible within your context, in order to gain insight and support. Join list serves or subscribe to newsletters from peace education organizations and networks. Reconciliation is by nature collaborative work!

5. *Trust in the process for the long run.* Resist discouragement even when your efforts seem to not have much of an effect. Reflect intentionally on your attempts to create a space for reconciliation and how students respond, keeping in mind that evaluating peacebuilding is a long-term process and measurement

is never exact. Trust that even small seeds planted today may bear fruit years from now.

CONCLUSION

For educators working for peace, there may be other paradigms and theories about what leads to reconciliation in addition to the five approaches listed above. Ultimately, it's not a matter of choosing one or the other, but actually all of the above. While we can't do everything in every class, an awareness of each of these approaches can help us broaden our work and infuse reconciliation into all aspects of our teaching and learning. As language educators, we know what is necessary in order for language learning to occur, but we can't say exactly when it happens that someone becomes fluent in a new language. In the same way, reconciliatory elements in English classes can direct people toward peace, though the actual moment when peace becomes a reality is a mystery. In the end, we can set up the space and do what we can as educators and learners, but it is God who does the work of transformation for reconciliation.

CHAPTER 2

INTERSECTIONS OF LANGUAGE LEARNING AND RECONCILIATION: NEW LANGUAGE, NEW VOICE

INTRODUCTION

My husband and I (Jan) had been married eight years when we took our first trip as a family to Brazil. Rod knew, of course, that I had grown up there and had occasionally heard me speak a little Portuguese with other family members. But I think he was unprepared for the transformation in my personality that started with my first taste of "cafezinho" and didn't end until we got back on the plane to return to Canada. Normally an introvert who feels drained at the end of a day full of people, in Brazil I was a regular socialite, mingling easily in social gatherings with little apparent stress. I happily made the smallest of small talk—something my husband knows that I normally struggle with. All of this prompted his comment one evening "Who are you, and what have you done with my wife?!"

Until that trip, returning to Brazil as an adult and morphing back into my Portuguese persona, I had not really considered the effect of language on identity, personality, and relationships. I became fascinated with the cultural differences inherent in languages, ultimately becoming convinced that there is untapped potential in using language learning as a catalyst for life growth, and specifically for growing past the limitations of one's home culture and sometimes even personality. I began to look at my English classes as opportunities for students to grow in many more ways than just English. I eventually focused on interaction between native and non-native English speakers in my dissertation, continuing to investigate how the language used in conversation affects the type and outcomes of the interaction and, subsequently, the relationships.

These experiences have ultimately led to co-authoring this book, along with the idea that *reconciliation* can be one of the additional outcomes of an English class. In this chapter, we introduce the premise that there are many natural connections between language acquisition and working towards reconciliation. We will first look at some underlying concepts about the nature of language, some realities of language acquisition, and opportunities inherent in language learning classrooms. Then, we will look at the practical application of these concepts, answering the question: *How does learning a new language provide someone with a new voice and context in which reconciliatory goals can be pursued?*

THE NATURE OF LANGUAGE

Anyone who has been involved in any kind of translation knows that some things just don't translate. Jokes, for instance, are frequently not funny in another language. Stories of cross-cultural miscommunication invariably have at their core a misunderstanding of a word or phrase; use of words which are appropriate in one language can become nonsensical, humorous, or offensive in another. A simplistic explanation for this could be that words have slightly different meanings in different languages, and nuances are hard to capture in translation.

However, there is likely more to the problem than simple differences in word meanings. The theory of linguistic relativity (See Kramsch, 1998) claims that language is not a neutral code that we use to communicate our ideas, but rather that the code itself affects our thought processes. It may limit the very ideas we are likely to have or promote certain ways of thinking about the world and people around us.

A very simple example can be found in the different ways in which Indonesian speakers and English speakers may view the color "pink." In Indonesian, the phrase for "pink" is "light red."

Red and pink have the same relationship in Indonesian that dark blue and light blue have in English. This may explain why I've been shown a whole range of fabrics which include pink, when asking for red fabric in a store in Indonesia. Certainly, the eyes of the Indonesian store clerks saw the same color that my eyes saw. But the words in our languages place these colors in different categories, and thus we "see" them differently. It is not too difficult to imagine that these different ways of thinking, imposed on us by our languages, could extend to far more consequential matters than colors.

Another relevant aspect about the nature of language, in relation to the theme of reconciliation, is the fact that its main purpose is communication. In years gone by, foreign language classes were often focused on learning grammar rules and translating readings. Today, however, most English language learning is undertaken for the purpose of *communication,* at least in theory! The approach of *communicative language teaching* (discussed more in chapter 7) is often the stated approach of English language classes, and most people don't feel they have "learned English" unless they can achieve some communication through English. The fact that communication is at the very heart of what it means to "know" a language is noteworthy when placed alongside the fact that communication is also at the very heart of peacebuilding and working towards reconciliation. Could it be that the journey towards effective communication in a new language naturally increases the potential for building peace and understanding? We believe that it may.

REALITIES OF SECOND LANGUAGE ACQUISITION (SLA)

Few human endeavors are as misunderstood as the nature of acquiring (or "learning") an additional language. Myths abound about how languages are learned. One such popular myth is that children pick up languages effortlessly and are much better at learning languages than adults. However, research shows that, given similar learning conditions, older children and adults can learn a new language just as quickly, and perhaps even more efficiently, than a young child (Lightbown and Spada 2013).[1] A more widespread understanding of the potential of adult learners to acquire a new language, and acquire it well, might increase the meaningfulness and hopefulness in adult language classrooms, and thus also increase their potential for reconciliation.

Another important concept about language acquisition is what Stephen Krashen (1981) called the *affective filter*, or our emotional state as we are learning. According to Krashen, a low affective filter is required for optimal language acquisition. That is, low-stress, peaceful environments are more conducive to language learning than stressful ones. This concept has obvious implications in a classroom designed to nurture peacebuilding! Pursuing goals of building understanding, acceptance, and peace can create an ideal classroom atmosphere for language acquisition.

Another relevant second language acquisition concept is the *language ego*. H. D. Brown claims that learning a new language involves developing new ways of "thinking, feeling, and acting—a second identity" (2001, 61). This new and different self can cause learners initially to feel uncertain and defensive. However, as beginning language learners gain confidence using their new language voice, the language ego can take a positive turn, resulting in an "alter ego" that is conducive to new growth and learning and that enables a new language speaker to step out of previous cultural confines. New English speakers have the potential of developing their "English-speaking self" as a slightly—or even significantly—different persona, just as I (Jan) did when I learned Portuguese and adopted a more "social" persona in the process. This issue of learner identity will be discussed more in chapter 5.

An additional concept which is a significant contributor to efforts at reconciliation in English language classrooms is the inextricable

---

[1] Children do have an advantage in one area: pronunciation. It is often their greater ability to sound like a "native speaker" that gives rise to the belief that children are better language learners, even though pronunciation is a relatively small part of language learning compared to the greater tasks of learning thousands of words, hundreds of grammatical structures, the ways in which language is used in various social contexts, and so much more.

link between language and culture (Kramsch 1998; Brown 2001). Learning a language also involves learning about cultural values and different ways of thinking. Successful language learners understand that using a new language may involve expressing ideas and feelings in very new and different ways. And the difference goes beyond different words, phrases, and expressions. Learning a new culture alongside a new language inevitably means "aha" moments as one becomes aware that there are ways of thinking about things that have never before been considered. I see this "aha" moment, for example, in English learners who suddenly realize that the typical absence of honorifics in American speech (e.g. calling people by their first names, even if they are older or in a position of authority) is not just "the way we do it here," but that it actually translates into a dearly held American cultural value of *equality.* The point here is that it is important to understand cultural values and the contexts they grew out of, and that this understanding can emerge through language learning.

A final second language acquisition concept that I will introduce here is the importance of *human interaction.* Any language teaching professional will tell you that pair and small group work is essential in a language classroom. Language learning requires language speaking, and without an abundance of small group activities, most classes simply cannot provide the amount of speaking time that language acquisition requires (see more about pair and small group work in chapter 7). Small group work is not just a logistical necessity, however. We attend to and are motivated by language that comes in the form of human interaction. Brain research has confirmed that human interaction is necessary for language learning. For example, in a study that looked at brain activity in infants when exposed to a new language spoken by a caregiver versus that same language heard on a CD, infants attended to the caregiver's language but not to the CD (Kuhl 2012). Without a doubt, the fact that we best acquire languages through human interaction is a powerful key to the goals of peacebuilding and reconciliation in language classrooms.

CHARACTERISTICS OF SECOND LANGUAGE CLASSROOMS

A final concept which sets the stage for reconciliation and peace-building in English language teaching relates to the nature of effective second language *classrooms.* The predominant goal in a language class is developing the skill to *use* the language for real communication, through reading, writing, speaking, and listening. Unlike a history or science class, where the goal may be to learn facts, a language class is more like a music class, where the goal is to learn a skill. For example, in a piano lesson, the goal is to learn to *play* the piano. There might be some theory, but mostly, if you are learning to play the piano, you spend lots of time playing the piano. In an English class, the *skill* being learned is using language for real communication. A fundamental error made in ineffective language classrooms is providing students with *information* (vocabulary and grammar rules) and assuming that *communication* will naturally follow. It normally does not. This is why successful language classrooms focus most of the class time on having students speak, listen, read, and write. The language classroom is a place of skill-building.

This emphasis on skill over information is also found in the field of Conflict Resolution in Education, which often specifically aims at building "critical life skills necessary for building caring communities and establishing constructive relationships" (Jones and Compton 2003). A change in behavior normally comes first before changing beliefs or larger social systems. In other words, we need to practice the skills of peace and reconciliation even before we fully understand the meaning behind these skills. This echoes the experience of language learning: we have to write in order to learn to write; we must speak in order to learn to speak.

Second language classrooms also focus on collaboration and community. In fact, a second language teaching approach of the 1970s was "Community Language Learning," an approach which aimed to provide a very low-stress, collaborative environment for acquiring a new language. Though community language learning as a strict methodology did not gain a wide following, elements of it have certainly fed into what is considered today to be an effective classroom learning environment; that is, one which is characterized by positive relationships, collaboration, and freedom to experiment and learn through trial and error. These qualities also characterize classrooms which are focused on conflict resolution and peacebuilding.

Language learning classrooms are characterized by *engagement*. Passive learning is not an option when learning a new language! Even the more "passive" skills of listening and reading are best characterized as "active listening" and "engaged reading." Here again, we find a useful parallel with Conflict Resolution Education, which also emphasizes active listening and full engagement in order to dismantle relational barriers and find respectful avenues for appreciation and dialogue.

Another quality of second language classrooms, which shares an affinity with the goals of peacebuilding and reconciliation, is the importance placed on practice. Learning to deal with conflict in healthy ways takes repeated effort at every opportunity. This consistent work at peacebuilding not only builds skills, but also transforms the relationships of those in conflict. Likewise, it is simply not possible to learn a language without using words and phrases again and again, until reaching a point of *automaticity*. The sheer abundance of talk required to truly develop skill and comfort in using a language usually means that the students in a class will get to know each other very well—whether they want to or not! As teachers present conversation tasks on everything from families to food preferences to disappointments to dreams for the future, students see into each other's lives more deeply than they ever anticipated. One adult English learner in Brazil commented about our Christian English program, "I came here to find English, and what I found was a new family!" She *did* learn English as well, but what overwhelmed her was how close she had gotten to the others in her English class, to the point of turning to them during a life crisis, rather than her family or church. Surely, the depth of relationship fostered by a good English class provides an essential foundation for doing the hard work of reconciliation and peacebuilding.

Finally, language classrooms often place unlikely people in close proximity. A young Korean front desk secretary sat in an English class made up of workers from the same office. In the hierarchical work culture of their company, it was extremely awkward for the boss and the secretary to be in the same class, and yet there they were. The young woman hardly spoke for the first class. However, as the course progressed, and communication skills and strategies were learned and practiced, the group became more comfortable speaking to each other in English and participating more actively in the lessons. After a few months, the young woman had become quite comfortable speaking to her boss both in English in class and even in Korean outside of class. Her boss seemed to enjoy hearing her perspectives and actually took her suggestions into consideration for the company. At one point they talked about this shift in relationship in the class. The boss said, "This would never have happened if it weren't for us learning a language together, where we're both at the same level." The secretary and boss in this story were not arch enemies needing reconciliation, but they certainly were from different social worlds with a cultural barrier preventing their friendship. Each developed a new voice in the English class: one of self-confidence and boldness for the secretary and one of unlikely and countercultural camaraderie for the boss. Each benefitted from the teacher's approach to teaching English that embraced possibilities for reconciliation and personal growth among unlikely participants, in the English class.

PRACTICAL APPLICATION: CONNECT LANGUAGE LEARNING TO THE SKILLS AND PRACTICES OF RECONCILIATION

1. *Utilize the new language to help students develop a new cultural lens.* Through the new language students may learn new ways of thinking about others, building empathy and understanding, and developing the skills to move between cultural lenses and different worldviews, depending on who they are interacting with.

2. *Consider that a new language may afford students the opportunity to create a new self.* The concept of "language ego," explains the phenomenon that language learning sometimes produces a type of "alter ego." We do not mean to suggest here that students' native languages, cultures, or identities are in need of replacing with an "English" version. Rather, as students become bilingual and bicultural, they have an *additional* communication vehicle through which to mediate new relationships. Since they now have an additional language choice, they may choose to use English for its ability to build more egalitarian relationships, for example.

3. *Teach students about communication.* Many people have never learned about communication as a field of study, and many have never had cause to examine the communication patterns in their native language. When learning a new language, however, one has to actively study these patterns. One learns about turn-taking, active listening, politeness, and even assertiveness. All these new skills dovetail with skills in reconciliation and peacebuilding.

4. *Provide opportunities to practice and hone respectful communication skills.* Classroom language learning is about nothing if not about practicing, practicing, practicing communication! Students in an English language classroom do not just learn about communication theoretically, in the abstract. Rather, they come to class day in and day out, with the main classroom activity being communication. Has a word been misused and a misunderstanding occurred? Never mind. There will be another chance tomorrow to correct the misunderstanding. Is one student reluctant to talk to another out of fear, distrust, or downright animosity? If the student stays in the class, chances are very high he will have to get over that reluctance and move into communication. By its sheer abundance, communication is eventually elicited from even reluctant speakers.

5. *Utilize the spaces that classroom language learning affords for dialogue across traditional boundaries.* English language classrooms are great equalizers. The need for English cuts across

social, educational, and professional boundaries. And English proficiency is no respecter of persons: a lowly messenger may well have better English than his boss with the big corner office several stories above him. Sometimes these individuals who would never otherwise cross paths find themselves face to face in an English class, and sometimes it is the messenger who excels in the language, not the big boss. While this dynamic can certainly cause tension, it also provides a beautiful opportunity to open up communication pathways with those whose lives rarely intersected before.

CONCLUSION

Sometimes we don't see the "fences" we place around our thinking and actions through the language we speak and the culture in which we live our lives. Learning a new language can help us create some gates in our fences where we can purposefully walk into a new space with new ways of thinking and relating to others. This is not to say that our own "backyard" language and culture are not good. We need to maintain them and return to them frequently. But being able to live and interact in new spaces can open up a world of possibilities, giving us a new voice.

CHAPTER 3

A FRAMEWORK FOR CHRISTIANS TEACHING ENGLISH FOR RECONCILIATION

INTRODUCTION

When I (Cheryl) first became interested in the area of English language teaching, I had a lot of questions about the field and what it would mean for me to teach with integrity from a Christian perspective. In one university course, I had a chance to look at the idea of teaching English as Christian mission more carefully and realized there were not a lot of resources available to help Christians sort through why they should be involved in teaching such a language of power. However, in Don Snow's book *English Teaching as Christian Mission* (2001) the chapter on teaching English for peacebuilding and intercultural understanding struck a chord. The framework of biblical peacebuilding in intercultural contexts somehow made sense of the concept of my involvement from a Christian perspective and, more broadly, the involvement of mission agencies in sending English teachers. This chapter seeks to expand on his ideas and those of the many writers and educators who have done significant reflection since then about why and how Christians English language teachers should think about teaching English for reconciliation.

The first two chapters of this book have outlined the field of teaching for reconciliation or peace and shown that language learning has a particular role in creating a new voice and providing opportunities for transformation and change. All of this is relevant to teachers of any faith background. So, what is particular about teaching for reconciliation for Christian English language teachers? Why should we pay attention to this in our teaching contexts? In the next few pages, we will point to several key theological concepts that can help us with these questions and suggest a framework for Christian teachers who wish to teach for reconciliation.

RECONCILIATION IN THE BIBLE

The Bible has a lot to say about peace and reconciliation. In the Bible, peace is a holistic concept which is often described as "shalom." Perry Yoder (1998) describes this as the central theme of the Bible and suggests that shalom can be defined as a concept that includes salvation, justice, and peace. This means peace is more than a lack of conflict, which is sometimes called "negative peace," and more closely connects with concepts of "positive peace," meaning an active effort toward creating peaceful societies, relationships, and environments even in the absence of violence or war. As Snow (2001) puts it, biblical peace is "a state of reconciliation" in which all sources of division "have been laid to rest." It is the breaking down of the dividing wall between God and people described in Ephesians 2:13–19 (NRSV):

> But now in Christ Jesus you who once were far off have been brought near by the blood of Christ. For he is our peace; in his flesh he has made both groups into one and has broken down the dividing wall, that is, the hostility between us. He has abolished the law with its commandments and ordinances, that he might create in himself one new humanity in place of the two, thus making peace, and might reconcile both groups to God in one body through the cross, thus putting to death that hostility through it. So he came and proclaimed peace to you who were far off and peace to those who were near; for through him both of us have access in one Spirit to the Father. So then you are no longer strangers and aliens, but you are citizens with the saints and also members of the household of God.

The dividing wall, or the hostility between us, is "put to death" and a new reality is established in its place.

This new reality pushes back against our tendencies to separate our relationship with God from our relationships with each other. It is Christ who has made both groups into one, which means that our reconciling with God is integrally connected with this process of reconciling with the other. It also means that our reconciliation with the other is a result of Christ's peace, whether we are "those who are near" or those "who were far off." This challenges our human tendencies to draw lines of division between what is spiritual and what is not, what is true peace and what is not. All peace is a gift from God through Jesus Christ, because he is the definition of "our peace" and created a new humanity from the brokenness of our human exclusions, limitations, and boundaries. This is a freeing peace, one that gives us the freedom of "citizens with the saints" and "members of the household of God" (Ephesians 2:19)!

The Bible is rich with stories of reconciliation and transformation of relationships between individuals, among communities, and between people and God. One could argue that the whole story of God's work in the world is an effort to reconcile the Creator with the created and people to each other. This "ministry of reconciliation" is described in detail in 2 Corinthians 5:17–20 (NRSV):

> So if anyone is in Christ, there is a new creation: everything old has passed away; see, everything has become new! All this is from God, who reconciled us to himself through Christ, and has given us the ministry of reconciliation; that is, in Christ God was reconciling the world to himself, not counting their trespasses against them, and entrusting the message of reconciliation to us. So we are ambassadors for Christ, since God is making his appeal through us; we entreat you on behalf of Christ, be reconciled to God.

We are called to live out the work of reconciliation with others because we have experienced this reconciliation through Christ. This work is not a prerequisite for reconciliation with God, but a joyous response to our experience!

This theme of God reaching out to draw all people into reconciliation, "not counting their trespasses against them," is threaded throughout the scriptures. When Adam and Eve disobey God in the garden, God provides clothing and a way for them to live. When Cain kills Abel and is cast out of his community, God provides safety and protection. When Joseph's brothers turn to violence, God cares for him and makes a way for the family to be reunited. When the Israelites are caught in oppression and slavery, God brings them out to freedom. When kings and rulers repeatedly turn away from God, God sends prophets and messengers to bring his people back. When God's people are desperate for his presence with them, he sends the Messiah to walk among them and lead the way back to right relationship with God. Time and again in the Bible people turn away from God—the God who continually seeks to make things right and to bring things to a place of "shalom."

The stories of Jesus in the New Testament continue with this theme but call us all to participate in this ministry of reconciliation. Jesus's birth, life and teachings, death, and resurrection all contain layers of meaning relating to reconciliation between God and people, as well as calling us to reconcile with one another. The Sermon on the Mount passages are often quoted as a focal point for peace theologians through which other teachings and stories of Jesus can be seen. It is clear that Jesus was not passive in his approach to peace, but actually quite radical in calling people to a new form of community and way of life which breaks down the barriers society establishes between people. His life models this as he eats with people from all strata of society, regularly interacts with women and marginalized people, and challenges others to see the traditions and laws of their culture differently. In Jesus's death, he models a nonviolent response to violence issued towards him, rather than violent retaliation, making a way for all people, even his enemies, to be reconciled with God and to each other.

The Bible also contains stories of followers of Jesus seeking to live at peace with each other and go beyond their own communities to break down dividing walls between people. A key story of this is the shift from ministry almost exclusively to the Jews to the inclusion of Gentiles in the early church community. While much conflict arose trying to figure out practically how this would work, New Testament writers consistently call people back to peace and unity (reconciliation) among themselves and with others (for example, see Col 3:15; 1 Thess 5:13; Rom 12:17–19; Heb 12:14).

Numerous other passages describe this relationship between humans and God and among people as both a blessing from God and something that we must work for by departing from evil and doing good; seeking peace, and pursuing it (Ps 34:14). In *Reconcile: Conflict Transformation for Ordinary Christians* (Lederach, Hybels, and Hybels 2014), peace practitioner John Paul Lederach uses Psalm 85, which poetically describes truth and mercy "kissing" and justice and peace "embracing" as a key metaphor for what reconciliation looks like in the Bible, both from a human perspective and between God and people. He suggests that all of these concepts—truth, mercy, justice, and peace—are part of reconciliation and actually give us deep insight into Christian approaches to building peace. Even with all these tools for peacebuilding, though, Lederach maintains that the moment of turning from facing away from each other in conflict to turning towards one another in reconciliation is a mystery. Our efforts can create the opportunity for this turning, but ultimately it is the work of the Holy Spirit present in our relationships and encounters that moves us in a new direction. Empowered with this Holy Spirit, Christians are called to the ministry of reconciliation in every facet of our lives. This ministry of reconciliation is our calling as followers of Jesus, who also assures us in the Sermon on the Mount that peacemakers will also be blessed, being called "the children of God" (Matt 5:9).

IMPLICATIONS FOR ENGLISH LANGUAGE TEACHING

So, Christians have many reasons to be involved in the work of reconciliation. As Christian English language teachers then, what does our position offer to this ministry? Snow (2001) suggests that a key part of our work is striving to both learn and teach intercultural understanding, seeking to break down stereotypes, increase empathy, reduce ethnocentrism, and expand our definition of "us" to include the other. This reflects Christ's incarnation—Christ with us—bridging the incredible cultural gap between divine and human, choosing to empty himself of the power of the divine culture in order to learn and walk with us in our human ways (Phil 2:7). Of course, we are not divine so we also need to work, perhaps primarily, on ourselves as agents of reconciliation in our teaching contexts—reconciled to God and to others, emptying ourselves of pride and self-righteousness in order to humbly learn and walk alongside those we serve through our teaching. This is perhaps the first step in teaching English for reconciliation.

However, in addition to this ongoing work of personal transformation, there can be some specific ways to intentionally work at creating our classrooms and interactions as spaces through which we invite God to give this gift of peace. Through these spaces, we can also learn about reconciliation, just like we can study about war and conflict. As we learn, discern, and pray about what this word means in our contexts, we can trust that the Holy Spirit will reveal to us how we can participate in God's ministry of reconciliation. The following framework is an attempt to articulate some ways to be intentional in our work.

This framework involves integration of three unique lenses (see Figure 1) with attention to the five approaches to teaching English for reconciliation mentioned in chapter 1. These lenses reflect the three fields that are integrated when teaching English for reconciliation. "Language" refers to the fields of TESOL and language acquisition, through which we can learn about the process of teaching and learning language. Looking through this lens helps us to keep a focus on the language learning experience and what will help learners achieve their language learning goals. It is very important that a "peace agenda" not trump a "language learning agenda"—the purpose for which learners have come to class. Such a diversion of class goals would result in a lack of integrity, and would never be a good basis for fostering reconciliation. (For more on the need for integrity in language teaching, see *Teaching English in Missions: Effectiveness and Integrity* by Dormer 2011.)

"Peace" refers to the fields of peacebuilding, peace education, conflict resolution in education, and other related areas that look at the study of what leads to reconciliation. Examining our teaching through this lens helps us to focus on strategies that are more likely to lead to peace and to reflect critically on how our actions may or may not lead to peace. "Faith" refers to theological and biblical study and practice rooted in Christian traditions. Looking through this lens helps us to connect with the spiritual element of reconciliation, providing the rationale for why we engage in this ministry of reconciliation and encouragement to continue the work. When planning lessons, curriculum, policy, classroom management, and other aspects of teaching, we can ask how this particular combination of lenses informs our approach.

FIG. 1: THREE LENSES OF A TEACHING ENGLISH WITHIN A RECONCILIATION FRAMEWORK

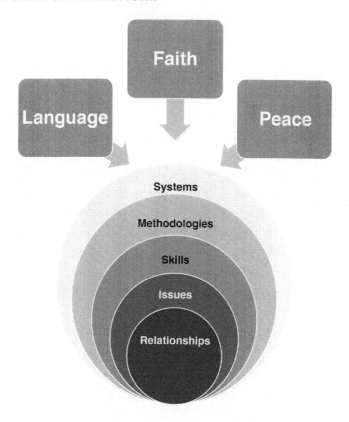

Christian English language teachers can engage this framework through reflective practice in seven areas, using the following questions as starting points:

1. *How can I develop my knowledge and experience of each lens and approach?* Christian English language teachers seeking to teach for reconciliation need to honestly assess their experience and training in all three areas—language, faith, and peace—in order not to risk doing unintentional harm to their learners or relationships in the community. Just as a lack of understanding about language teaching means that students will not get the best support in acquiring a new language, a lack of knowledge and experience from a faith lens can result in misunderstandings and miscommunication regarding spiritual issues. A lack of peace knowledge can result in harming relationships or escalating conflicts. Detailed training is available for a variety of peacebuilding topics such as restorative justice, trauma healing, organizational health, strategic change, community development, facilitation and group dynamics, and many others, all of which can provide great insight to creating space for reconciliation in the classroom context. While this book introduces some of these concepts in the following chapters, each is a field in its own right and language teachers could benefit from exploring those that interest them in more depth. Just as language teachers need ongoing professional development in the field of language teaching and acquisition, so do teachers for reconciliation need lifelong learning about peace.

2. *How can I promote learner participation, respect, and empowerment through each lens and approach?* Reconciliation is a very personal matter, even when taking place between groups of people. It cannot be forced or directed by someone who is outside of the broken relationship. In many peacebuilding situations, conflict has erupted due to certain voices being suppressed, disempowered, or at least left out of decision-making processes. James Gilligan (2001), a psychiatrist working with violent offenders in prison systems in the United

States, asserts that shame is at the heart of all acts of violence, individual or collective. Respect and empowerment can counter this shame and provide tools for support for people who experience shame to find ways to respond other than in violence. Even if students have not directly been involved in physical violence, other less obvious forms of violence can have a big impact on them. Cultural and structural violence may be at play in the lives of language learners who are often navigating issues of employment, class mobility, language oppression, or other difficult and complex forces that may leave them feeling frustrated and ashamed. Learner participation and empowerment is essential in countering these forces in our societies and student lives, helping to create a space conducive to peace.

3. *How can I nurture community and healthy relationships through each lens and approach?* Creating a space for reconciliation requires that the space is also relatively safe and a positive place that learners want to come to. We can never guarantee that a space is safe for everyone, and if we claim that we have created a safe space, harm done feels even more hurtful against the expectation of safety. However, we can create a positive space where we set expectations and actively nurture ways of communicating, interacting, telling jokes, giving feedback, and helping each other that build each other up and make everyone in the classroom feel more positive by the end of class. This question also extends outside of class to the ways that teachers interact with students' parents or other teachers and model the extension of this positive environment beyond the classroom walls.

4. *How does my and the learners' culture and identity influence each lens and approach?* While demographics on paper are important to know, there is much more involved in culture and identity interactions in the classroom than simply what language people speak or what country they come from. Cultural groups are not only dynamic and fluid, but individuals also interact with culture in unique ways given other aspects of their identities and personalities. As teachers, we need to recognize that our identities and cultures are also shifting and

changing in interactions within the classroom and to reflect on how this might influence student perceptions of the teacher, the other students, and the overall environment. This question will be addressed more in chapter 5.

5. *How do my worldview and the learners' worldviews shape how we use each lens and approach?* This question builds on the inquiry into culture and asks about the narratives and assumptions that we bring into the classroom regarding the way the world works. While these are often cultural, they also vary greatly from person to person. One way to start hearing others' worldviews is to listen to the metaphors people use to talk about their experiences. Do students talk about learning a language as a hurdle to overcome while the teacher speaks of it as an opportunity to grow? Neither of these metaphors is wrong, but they represent different worldviews which may lead to conflict. If this teacher gives an assignment like a journaling task, for example, and gives general feedback rather than specific details of what is right and wrong, students trying to get over their hurdle might feel that it is a waste of time and become quite frustrated with the task.

6. *What opportunities for transformation or positive change in relation to each lens and approach are happening for me and the learners individually, collectively, or in our contexts?* One way to pay attention to this question is to communicate with students about this when and if it is appropriate. It is important not to assume what is happening in other people's lives based on our perspective or observations alone. Checking in with others about where they are and talking about what we observe, including affirming and validating positive change along the way, is essential for supporting this transformation, whether in language learning, relationships, peacebuilding, or spiritual aspects. Of course, this question is asked while also keeping culture, identity, and worldview in mind.

7. *How are our spirits or creativity being stirred by God's Spirit at work among us through each lens and approach?* An essential aspect of teaching English for reconciliation is nurturing our

creative spirits, which is so important in working for peace. Not only do we need creativity to try to think outside the ways in which conflict has been perpetuated for so long, we also need to find creative ways to sustain ourselves and others in the work of being peacemakers. Watching for God's Spirit at work among us can bring us a renewed sense of purpose and joy in the difficult task of being agents of reconciliation when we often cannot see results of the work we do.

PRACTICAL APPLICATION—INTEGRATING THE FRAMEWORK INTO YOUR TEACHING

1. *Ground your teaching in the bigger picture.* Reconciliation doesn't happen in one class period. Remember that your efforts are part of God's larger ministry of reconciliation and give thanks for opportunities to participate. Focus on aligning your work with God's call to peace rather than looking for measurable change after each lesson.
2. *Post reminders of each lens to see when you plan lessons.* Print the figures or list of questions to have with you when you're planning your classes or create your own lists or images that help you keep each lens in mind.
3. *Experiment and evaluate freely.* Try out new approaches in your class and reflect on the outcome. Assess how your experiments have gone from the perspective of each lens and make decisions about what to do differently the next time.
4. *Pray about reconciliation in your context.* Share your work with your church community and invite them to join you in praying for wisdom in understanding what reconciliation looks like in your teaching context.

CONCLUSION

We hope that this framework will spark ideas, prompt reflection, and help shape a vision for teaching English for reconciliation. We hope that the suggestions provided here will enable you to focus intentionally on creating opportunities and spaces for the ministry of reconciliation. Overall, we can be assured that reconciliation is God's work and we can participate freely, knowing that God will use what we offer in a spirit of humility and service. In the midst of this, we can learn about what fosters reconciliation and be more intentional about that in our teaching. At the very least, we are closer to doing no harm and at best, allowing God to work through our efforts as the one "who by the power at work within us is able to accomplish abundantly far more than all we can ask or imagine" (Eph 3:20, NRSV).

PART 2

THE PEOPLE:
WHO IS INVOLVED IN TEACHING
ENGLISH FOR RECONCILIATION?

CHAPTER 4

COMMUNITY

INTRODUCTION

I (Jan) had worked in Indonesia for many years, teaching English in both Christian and Muslim schools, when I had a brainstorm for a peacebuilding project. I wanted to have the junior high students in a Christian school spend a couple of hours with junior high students in a nearby Muslim school. I knew both of these schools well. I had taught in the Muslim school for three years, and I had worked with the Christian school for about ten years, mostly in teacher training.

My idea was to form pairs of students—one Christian and one Muslim—to work on an English project together. The goal would be for them to become friends, then do an English activity together in which they would discuss their differences and commonalities. Knowing the two groups of students, I thought they would find many commonalities, and that all students would, at the end of the day, come to see the other group in a more compassionate light. I even hoped that some would want to be Facebook friends and that the divisions between these two groups might be lessened. I have provided many teacher training seminars with both Christians and Muslims in attendance in that part of Indonesia, and have generally witnessed goodwill and friendship between these two groups. So, I felt that this project had a very good chance of being warmly embraced by both schools.

I first approached a representative from the Muslim school. "No problem," she said. "That will be good for them." Great! I had thought the Muslim school would pose the biggest barrier, so with the endorsement from them, I enthusiastically began planning the event while waiting for a response from the principal of the Christian school. But the response from the Christian school stopped me in my tracks . . . not only in planning the project, but in my thinking about Christian schools. "*I* like this idea a lot" the principal said, "and I think it would be very good for the students. But," she continued, "I'm worried about the parents. They won't want their children to go into a Muslim school."

This was a twist that I had not expected. I had assumed that parents who were quite happy for their children to memorize "love your neighbor" in school would naturally be keen on the expression of that being a visit to a Muslim school. There may have been complexities surrounding that situation that I, as a foreigner, did not grasp, and I was not able to engage in the dialogue which could have helped me understand their concerns. The project never developed, much to the loss of the students and teachers in both schools.

We use this story to introduce the crucial role that the larger *community* plays in reconciliatory efforts. In this second part of the book we are focusing on the *who* of reconciliation. Who contributes to the processes of peacebuilding and conflict resolution? In this first chapter in the section, we look at the power and importance of the community. Since English language teaching contexts are so varied, the communities which surround them are also quite varied, and it would be impossible to address each type of community which could play a role in an English-learning context. Here, we will focus on three broad communities: the society, the family, and the school.

THE SOCIETY

The first difficulty inherent in discussing the role of society in efforts to teach English for reconciliation comes in defining the word "society." Everyone lives within multiple geographical societal circles, such as neighborhoods, villages, cities, states, and countries. These societies exert varying forces on individual thoughts, actions, and choices, depending on the nature of local culture, government, and politics. Individuals also live and work within various other communities, such as those stemming from religious and professional affiliations Sometimes these types of communities exert much more influence over individuals than the geographical communities within which they reside. In the story above it was, interestingly, not the Muslim-majority country that proved to be a barrier in building relationships across religious boundaries, but rather the local Christian community norms and perspectives—shaped no doubt by their position as a minority amidst the dominant Muslim culture.

"Know your students" is one of the most important dictums for teachers of English. We need to know their language proficiency levels, first languages, cultural backgrounds, learning preferences, and much more. We should add to this list the need to know the larger community within which they are learning English. This may not only be a geographical location. For example, a Saudi student studying English in the United States is usually still very much influenced by Saudi and Muslim society. He is likely receiving a scholarship from the Saudi government to study in the US, and that scholarship comes with many strings attached. We need to know both the allowances and restrictions that this student faces.

Likewise, an immigrant in Canada may identify much more with the community of immigrants from the same country than with Canadian society at large. For example, in the story shared in the introduction, students knew very little about Canadian society and did not yet feel a part of it. Their concern lay with the community of refugees from the former Yugoslavia and the animosity and strife within that community.

So, our first order of business as teachers is simply to know as much as we can about the communities impacting our students. Various ways of knowing these communities might be possible, such as asking students (and others) questions, attending local community events and reading newspapers and other local publications. In my (Jan's) experience, simply showing an interest opens many doors. I am inclined to think that the fact that the Muslim school welcomed the initiative I shared at the beginning of this chapter was due to my presence in that school for three years and the continued interest I demonstrated in learning about their community. I was not one of them; they knew and respected that I was a Christian. But my genuine interest in their practices and beliefs led to deep trust. They knew I would not suggest something for their students that would not be beneficial for them.

Sometimes we can go a step beyond acquiring knowledge, and actually work with individuals in a community, to build bridges of understanding and to further reconciliatory goals. It may be possible to include individuals in a community in English-learning endeavors by, for example, inviting a community representative to class as a special speaker, or by having students document information about their communities for an English learning project. For example, in one intensive English program class made up of a variety of international students and local immigrant participants, I (Cheryl) collaborated with a local high school social studies teacher who was working on a unit about migration and movement in history. He had the high school students create questions they had about people who come to the US, then sent them to our class. My students chose several of the questions and put together videos for the high school students to watch. Afterwards, the high school students wrote a short response which was shared with our class. For many of them, it was an eye-opening experience to read about the variety of stories that immigrants and visitors to the US could have. Several mentioned that stereotypes they had of people from other countries had been challenged.

Finally, we can actively teach the concept of *community* in our English classes. English language texts and curricula typically have units or chapters on the community. At low English proficiency levels, students learn words for places in the community, such as the grocery store, the library, and the doctor's office. Students practice dialogues for these various places in their communities, such as asking where certain items are located in a grocery store or telling a doctor about their health symptoms. At higher levels, students can investigate their own community circles and identify ways in which they are influenced by their communities. This can result in more clarity in their thinking about life choices and can also lead them towards thinking about how they can have a positive influence in their communities.

In my own (Jan's) writing of materials for English learning, I have always loved coming to the topic of *community*, and utilizing it in my materials to help students grow and learn in multiple ways. In my *English for Life* curriculum (Dormer 2011; also available through my website; see Appendix C), a five-level task-based curriculum, level three (low intermediate-level proficiency) is entirely devoted to the topic of community. The tasks at this level begin with having students identify and learn places in their communities and conversations which would occur in them, but move beyond this passive knowledge to active engagement in the community through a volunteering project. I also wrote two textbooks for a Christian English as a Foreign Language (EFL) series for children (Dormer 2012, 2013; see information about the *Passport to Adventure* series in Appendix C). In these texts as well, children are led beyond a passive learning about community to identify ways of active engagement within the community, such as through a recycling project.

All of these strategies for including the community—gaining knowledge, inclusion, and active teaching—lead to a perspective that blurs the boundaries between classroom and community. Reconciliation of any type is not likely to happen within the classroom without understanding, respect, and appreciation for the values, perspectives, and beliefs that exist outside the classroom and that exert powerful forces on the students.

THE FAMILY

The greatest external influence on many students, including adult learners, is their family. The concept of "family" has many diverse interpretations in different cultures, including differences in who can make decisions about what, the level of support provided to family members, and the extent to which external events such as a move to a new country affect family dynamics. Differences notwithstanding, families figure prominently in how most of us conduct our lives, and this is no less true for English learners.

K–12 (KINDERGARTEN–GRADE 12) CONTEXTS

Of course, where family is concerned, there is a big difference between teaching children and teaching adults. So, we will first address here some issues related to teaching children and working with their parents. Then, we will go on to talk more generally about the importance of building family relationships and teaching communication skills.

When I (Jan) speak to groups of K–12 teachers and broach the subject of working with parents, I often hear a collective groan, no matter the country I am speaking in. Teachers around the world are all too familiar with the scenario of a parent complaining about a grade, or making demands concerning curricula or requirements. In all fairness, I have probably been the cause of a few teacher groans myself, as I did on more than one occasion darken a teacher's door to let my thoughts be known regarding my daughters' education.

That confession aside, I have much more often been on the other side of the equation, as a teacher myself, or working with teachers and school leaders who were confronted with sometimes unrealistic and uninformed parental demands. This is especially common where language acquisition is concerned. Second language acquisition is one of those areas in which everyone fancies themselves an expert. As was mentioned in chapter 2, for example, most people believe that children pick up languages easily, and many people cannot really be convinced otherwise. So, parents of children who are in schools or classes designed to help them learn English may have false expectations and ideas about what their children need.

Such thinking was evident among parents in a school in Indonesia. The school claimed to be a bilingual school but, in fact, was trying to teach all subjects in English, which is a full immersion model and not a bilingual model (Dormer 2017). I met with school leaders, teachers, and the school board (none of whom had any training in education) and urged them to teach at least one subject fully in Indonesian. I suggested the subject of Bible. I explained how research shows only positive outcomes when the native language continues to be developed in school. I explained the fact that we have abundant research showing that students with higher first language development do better, both academically and in second language development. The school director was convinced, and she made immediate plans to begin to change all the Bible classes to an Indonesian curriculum. I left the school quite pleased with this progress.

But my satisfaction was short-lived. Only weeks later I heard that parents had risen up in revolt. Their worry? That their children would now learn English less perfectly because the school was not fully in English. I thought to myself, "I'll just go there and talk to the parents, and all will be well." But all was *not* well during that fateful meeting with parents. They did not believe the research which shows superior English learning when children also develop their native language. When this argument was cast aside, I had one last card up my sleeve which I thought for sure would cause them to reconsider. "Don't you want your children to learn Bible in their heart language? Don't you want them to be prepared for Christian ministry here in Indonesia?" "No!" was the startling reply. The parents went on to tell me that they wanted their children to go abroad and did not envision a future for them in Indonesia. Soon after that unproductive confrontation I found out that the school director—the one who had believed in my ideas—had been terminated, due to parental demand.

There is much we could discuss regarding reconciliation in relation to this unfortunate event, not the least of which might be to call Christian schools to a higher commitment to developing students who care about making a difference within their own countries. But what can this story tell us about working with parents? I spent many hours thinking through what went wrong at that school, and always came back to two key ingredients of good relationships: time and respect. The parents were not given time to process the new idea before it was implemented. I misunderstood the role of the parents in the school, believing that the director had more authority and support than she did, and so I encouraged her decision to make changes, assuming the parents would eventually see the benefit of the decision. Had the idea been introduced slowly and changes not been made until the majority were on board, there could have been a very different outcome.

I realize also, now as I look back, that I lacked respect for the parents' position. It's easy for me to urge Indonesian parents to envision a future for their children in Indonesia, where they can make a difference, when my own daughters are well-settled with good jobs in the United States. How do I know that I would not want the same thing for my child, were I in their shoes? Ultimately, I have had to accept what happened at that school as a failure on my part to adequately listen to and respect those parents. I do still believe that a different decision would have been better for the students. Respect is not about who is right and who is wrong. Had I afforded them the respect and listening ear that they deserved, I would have understood their realities much better, and might have been able to suggest baby steps towards a more effective program, such as having the Bible classes only partially in Indonesian.

The take-away here is that reconciliation may be needed between school personnel and parents. The rift between these two may be due to parents not understanding what teachers understand about education, but it can also happen because teachers don't know what parents know about their children. Either way, this rift has a negative impact on the children involved, and we as teachers need to seek reconciliation with parents by building strong relationships with them and using effective communication skills, two issues which were addressed in chapter 1. These efforts, combined with an attitude and actions of respect, can pave the way toward working together for the good of our students and *modeling* for them the very nature of reconciliation.

ALL ENGLISH LEARNING CONTEXTS

We now shift our attention from K–12 education to all English teaching settings. Contributing whatever we are able to the building of strong family relationships should be an underlying goal for all Christians. In English classes, we have spectacular opportunities to do this. Just as the topic of "community" is prominent in English language curricula, so is the topic of "family." In fact, in beginner-level English language lessons, students learn the words for family relationships. As students learn more, they are often asked to talk about their families, telling about physical characteristics, personalities, hobbies, and habits.

English class activities on the topic of family can include discussions on helping one another, forgiving one another, and supporting one another. Students can be given tasks to interview family members, and even if family members do not speak English, students can conduct the interview in the native language, then report back to class in English. One student who was given such an assignment discovered how badly her mother felt when the daughter made fun of her pronunciation of English words. This conversation may never have taken place without an assignment for English class. Through this assignment, a wound was shared, empathy created, and greater sensitivity and respect was the result.

Sometimes, whole English programs or courses can be designed specifically for strengthening families. One approach to language teaching that we will learn more about in chapter 7 is *Content-Based Language Teaching* (CBLT): learning English while studying something else. When immigrant children in American schools learn English because their teacher is teaching them math in English, CBLT is at work. When children in Germany are in a bilingual school in which they learn science in English, CBLT is at work. And in an English-medium cooking class for women in Japan, CBLT is also at work. In each of these cases, the focus of the class is something other than English—math, science, or cooking. But because the teaching happens in English, the English language is also acquired.

My husband and I (Jan) created a CBLT course on the Christian family for our seminary in Brazil. Our course content included family dynamics, child development, child rearing, family devotions, and marital relationships. As the teaching and materials were all in intermediate-level English, our students developed English skills alongside the course content. Most of the individuals in the course did not attend specifically because they wanted to learn about the family. Rather, they wanted to improve their English. This course was presented to them as an option. They had never heard of a CBLT course before, but they decided to try it and got much more than they bargained for. One father said with tears in his eyes that he now knew some things he had been doing wrong in raising his son. Another young woman reported having some deep conversations with her fiancé, which altered and strengthened the course of their relationship.

We have talked about relating to parents and about building strong family relationships. A final idea to consider here is the possibility of actively teaching effective communication skills to whole families. In chapter 1 we mentioned that one problem in teaching communication skills in English classrooms is that students need to use these skills with individuals who have *not* learned effective communication strategies. For example, a sixth-grader in an English class may learn active listening and turn-taking skills. She may then try to use these skills with her parents, who are taken aback by her statement "What I hear you saying is . . ." and who feel that this sounds just a bit smug coming from their child! One possibility in some contexts is to offer workshops for the *whole family* on effective communication. This can be framed as an English-learning workshop for the whole family, where the topic will be effective communication. Another way to provide some understanding of good communication skills for family members of the English student is to embed these ideas in homework practice. Students can be given a script to practice at home with a parent or sibling. Though such practice is not overt teaching on communication, it can plant seeds by demonstrating good conversational styles. I (Cheryl) worked with kindergarten children and their mothers in Korea, learning English together while discussing cultural perspectives of family and child-rearing. Although the mothers did mention that the content was helpful, they all commented that the most important outcome of the class was the transformation of their relationships with their children!

No matter what our English teaching context or role, there are likely some steps we, as English teachers, can take to strengthen family relationships.

The School

A school is a community unlike any other! If you work in any kind of school, be it elementary, high school, university, an English school, or even a Sunday school, you will know what I mean. As is true in any human endeavor where there are positions and opinions and requirements and responsibilities, things sometimes don't go according to plan—people mess up, and harmony does not always prevail. School environments can bring out the very best and the very worst in people and are *always* places where God's grace is needed in abundant supply.

Yet schools have the teaching focus that is lacking in the geographical community and the intentionality that may be lacking in the family community, which makes them prime places where individuals can learn, experience, and practice reconciliation and peace education. Depending on the cultures and structures of the school and surrounding societies, peace education programs may go by different names or have slightly different goals. All of them, though, work to create a better, more just and peaceful world. There are generally three ways to include peace education in a formal educational setting. One way is to focus on peace as a separate topic, such as in a peace club or a conflict resolution class. Another way is to integrate it into each class, training teachers to include skills, topics, and methods of peace education in history, mathematics, social studies, and other subjects. A final way is to infuse it into the curriculum as part of the paradigm of the school, which means considering how every aspect of the school's policies and structures support peace, such as with restorative justice in education (Amstutz and Mullet 2005).

Whether through separate topics, integration, or infusion, English classes or programs can benefit from and influence the larger school community through a focus on reconciliation. The following examples describe a couple of ways of doing this.

First, we will look at the context of English learners in English-medium (English-speaking) K–12 schools. All too often, English learners are left out or forgotten in school initiatives. For example, one school began a peer mediation project, inviting all classes to send two students to peer mediation training. That is ... all classes were invited *except* the English as a Second Language (ESL) class. The reasoning was, of course, that the ESL students would not understand the training. The English learners may indeed have struggled with the language, but in this day where translation can be accessed at the touch of a screen, there are certainly ways to communicate this vital training in other languages. The training of English learners as peer mediators could have significant benefits in the school, in terms of providing mediation in other languages, and having peer mediators who are already adept at cross-cultural communication.

So, the first thing to remember is that good initiatives in the school at large that foster communication, relationship-building, and reconciliation should apply to and filter into ESL classes as well. But the fact is that in many school systems, perhaps most around the world, intentional teaching and practicing of reconciliatory skills does not take place. It is in these systems that English classes can lead the way, promoting and modeling practices which would provide a school-wide benefit

For example, imagine a Christian international high school in Asia. The language of the school is English, and the school utilizes an American curriculum. However, 80 percent of the students are English learners. In an effort to increase the use of English on campus and to increase integration of the students from differing native languages, the school has instituted a strict "English only" policy. However, tension surrounds this policy. Students sometimes use their native languages out of rebellion, as teenagers often do. And the policy seems to have had no effect on the cliques formed around native language use—perhaps even intensifying them—so teachers and staff at the school are frustrated. The school is in need of reconciliation on multiple levels—between students who speak different native languages, and between the school administration and the students who are "pushing back" against the English-only policy.

Consider the possible influence of a thoughtful and knowledgeable ESL teacher with a goal of bringing about understanding, healing, and change. Only some of the students who are defying the English-only policy are in ESL classes. The others are highly proficient in English and are not in the ESL program. Still, the ESL teacher believes that the ESL classes may provide a context for needed dialogue. She begins by assigning research, writing, and speaking tasks on the topic of language use. The ESL students begin to see the power of language as they investigate language rights, identities, sociocultural language use, and issues of inclusion and exclusion through language. The teacher further has her students investigate language use through the lens of Scripture. Students are tasked with responding to a prompt on how their own choice and use of languages reflects biblical principles. They are also charged with reflecting on how the school's language policy may or may not reflect Christian principles.

The ESL students begin talking with their friends about their discoveries regarding language. The ESL teacher informs the head of school about the project, opening the door for staff dialogue on language use and the school's language policy. Eventually, the ESL teacher is invited to present a workshop for the teachers on the topics of language rights, translanguaging,[2] stress factors in second language acquisition, and other topics related to the English learners in the school. A committee is formed to reconsider the language policy and to consider other approaches that could foster integration and minimize language cliques. What began as reconciliatory efforts in a small ESL class eventually came to impact the whole school. (For more on creating a positive multilingual school environment, see the book *What School Leaders Need to Know about English Learners,* Dormer 2016.)

In many parts of the world, English as a foreign language (EFL) classes in regular schools can also have a significant effect on the school community. I (Jan) experienced this when I taught English in a very low-resource elementary school. The students in that

---

[2] "Translanguaging" is a relatively new term for the purposeful use of two or more languages in communication. Whereas the term "code-switching" has sometimes been viewed negatively, translanguaging sees linguistic prowess and resourcefulness in the use of two or more languages.

school had mostly experienced rote learning. The classroom was not a place which fostered good relationships. Teachers were stern, and both teacher-student and student-student relationships were sometimes abusive. In my English class I introduced pair and group work. This was quite difficult at first, as students only seemed to have *group* control. *Self*-control had not been well-developed. So, I experienced quite a lot of misbehavior when I began to ask students to work together in pairs. Over time, however, students began to learn and practice respectful dialogue. Other teachers would sometimes come into my class to watch my strange methods. These eventually filtered into other classroom spaces. It was a pure joy to return years later and see many more smiles and a much higher level of interaction than I remembered when I had first stepped onto the school grounds ten years prior.

Programs for adults, whether in private English schools, universities, or community colleges, can also be intentional in fostering the kind of community in which reconciliatory work could occur. I (Jan) taught an intensive English program in a large American university that had many Saudi students. Many of the other instructors in the program were young graduate assistants who had no previous interaction with Muslims and who seemed to the Muslim students not to appreciate their religious practices or culture. The Muslim students soon learned that I viewed them differently, due to many years interacting with Muslims in Indonesia, and the students expressed their concerns to me. I was able to initiate dialogue among the staff, which did not result in an immediate change in perspective, but which did begin the process of increasing religious and cultural awareness for all the staff. Further, I felt that greater understanding among *all* student groups was needed, so I secured hallway bulletin board space on which students from different cultures and religions could present their beliefs and traditions. I incorporated an oral presentation of the bulletin board into an English-speaking assignment in my beginning conversation class. I will never forget the Saudi student who had led the students in airing complaints beaming as he presented the cultural and religious information on the Saudi bulletin board to a small group of students and teachers. A space for dialogue had been opened up in the program, and understanding and appreciation for different ways and beliefs grew from there.

All school communities, whether public or private, whether for adults or children, can benefit from intentionality in creating spaces where different voices can be heard and appreciated and where respectful dialogue becomes the norm.

PRACTICAL APPLICATION: INCLUDING THE COMMUNITY IN RECONCILIATORY EFFORTS

1. *Know and respect the various societal communities which influence your students.* Avoid the tendency of thinking about the English classroom as an isolated, self-contained space, and instead seek out connections between the English class and the larger community. This can be done through consultation with community representatives, inviting guest speakers to class, and creating English-learning projects which are based in the community.

2. *If you teach children, actively cultivate good relationships with their parents.* If possible, spend time listening to their realities and concerns about their children. Don't expect parents to automatically accept what you, the educational expert, say. Rather, respect their opinions and ideas, gently making suggestions which may nudge them towards a greater understanding of educational, language-learning, and communication concepts.

3. *Work in whatever ways you are able to strengthen families.* Consider making "family" a prominent topic in the English class, and be sure to move on from simple descriptions to actually talking about relationships and communication. Assign homework that will promote family dialogue and model effective ways of communicating.

4. *Engage in purposeful activities to expand efforts towards reconciliation into the larger school context.* Consider whether separate, integrated, or infused peace programs might be a good fit for your context. Ensure that ESL/EFL students are included

in any school-wide peace or mediation initiatives. Be alert for any relational barriers or tensions due to language or culture, and take the lead in addressing these issues through the use of reconciliatory principles.

CONCLUSION

An English teacher in nearly any English teaching context can have influence that goes beyond the English classroom itself. There may be ways to impact the community, the families represented by the students, and certainly the school itself, with the practices and hope of reconciliation.

CHAPTER 5

LEARNERS

INTRODUCTION

One semester I (Cheryl) taught the same course in two back-to-back time periods. The two groups of students looked identical on paper. They were mostly graduate students taking the advanced writing course as a requirement for their graduate studies programs. Most of them had bursaries paid for by their departments, so there were high expectations for attendance, participation, and completion of assignments. Students were in the same age range and from the same variety of language backgrounds, and neither group of students knew each other before they arrived in class. The levels were the same, the textbook was the same, my lesson plans were the same . . . but the classes were completely different!

It was amazing to watch, and I tried to pin down the variables that made them such different groups. Was one group a little stronger than the other in academic writing? Did the time of day make such a difference? The only thing I could discern was that the learners were different people: I responded to them differently and they interacted with each other differently. Identity made all the difference. Subsequently the class dynamics were different too. At first, I thought I would have difficulty remembering with which class I did what, but in reality, it was as clear to me as if I had been teaching two completely different subjects. I never had any problem remembering who was in which class because each dynamic was so unique, and that group dynamic colored all we did.

This is the power of identity—not just the demographic information about learners, but the constantly shifting, changing, moving system of *identities* of learners and teacher in the classroom. Student and teacher identity has become a key topic in TESOL and applied linguistics in the last few decades (Norton 2016; Taylor 2013). Identity is often defined in the context of relationship. Who am I? A teacher (in relation to students), a writer (in relation to readers), a mother (in relation to my children), a friend (in relation to other friends), or a language learner (in relation to the language and speakers of that language). In other words, identity is "the way a person understands his or her relationship to the world, how that relationship is structured across time and space, and how the person understands possibilities for the future" (Norton 2013). All of these aspects of identity can shift depending on where, when, and with whom one is interacting.

This chapter explores the complexity of learner identities in relation to teaching English for reconciliation. After discussing aspects of students' personal and collective identities in the language classroom, and the ways in which these identities interact, we will provide some practical tools to guide language teachers in paying attention to identity in order to contribute to peace and reconciliation within the classroom community.

UNDERSTANDING LEARNER IDENTITIES

How do learner identities relate to teaching English for reconciliation? In essence, identities are at the center of our work. Whenever we use language to communicate, our identities play a part. Indeed, who we are shapes the language we choose to use, the access we have to language variations, and the opportunities we have to use and learn languages (Norton and Toohey 2011). So, our communication is rooted in the social networks that surround us. These networks are also the places where conflict happens. Much of conflict revolves around identity issues, reflected in the questions "Who am I and who gets to say who I am?" When people coming from conflict zones meet together, like the story told in the introduction of the students coming from different sides of the

Yugoslav war into an English class, these identities that have been at the fore so long are sometimes hard to put aside. When we do put them aside, it is because other aspects of our identities have become more important . . . important enough to turn to face the "other" and commit to a new kind of relationship. This transformation reflects a shift of our definition of self in relation to others—essentially, our identity—which happens through communication and is expressed through our language.

COLLECTIVE IDENTITIES

The groups that we are a part of—our "collective identities"—profoundly shape who we are and how we relate to others. These are often our communities, and as described in chapter 4, we as teachers need to learn about and consider the people, institutions, and cultures of learners' communities when planning English classes and programs. However, it is not just the people of the surrounding community we need to consider. It is also the effect this group has on how learners define themselves. National borders, for example, are often used to define learners, but this may or may not be one of their primary collective identities. Ethnic or regional boundaries may actually be more powerful than national ones for some students. Also, the group that we primarily identify with can change depending on who we are with. For example, someone from South Korea might strongly differentiate themselves as "Korean" when interacting with Japanese and Chinese classmates, but align themselves just as strongly with "Asians" when interacting with classmates from North America. Similarly, other aspects of identity such as gender, age, or religion can play a role in collective identities. A female student from the Middle East may in one grouping identify more as "female" and in another grouping identify more as "Muslim." And older students may define themselves differently than younger students of the same ethnic origin. This dynamic of self-identifying with different collective identities based on who is in the room is often quite evident in the language classroom and probably accounts for quite a bit of the difference I (Cheryl) experienced in my two classes.

Another powerful dynamic of collective identities is in- and out-group thinking. Naturally, we tend to categorize people into groups of "us" and "them." Some researchers think this is a way to recognize and keep track of close family and friends and to pay attention to who is safe and who is not. This protects us from unknown dangers, but it also helps us conserve our energy and focus on the relationships most meaningful to us. On the other hand, the resulting "othering" can easily become quite rigid and even antagonistic. Particularly when harm has come from the outside at some point and this trauma has become a part of a person's way of seeing themselves and the world, it is easy to demonize the other and build strict boundaries for self-protection. This can sometimes result in continuing the cycle of violence by acting in ways that harm the other out of a desire for self-defense.

In the language classroom, some of these in- and out-groups may be in place long before class begins, based on previous experiences, identities, prejudice, and stereotypes. It is important for teachers to be aware of the identities students bring into the class, but also to reserve judgment, realizing that identity is complex, and we may only see a small part of it. For example, in one class, I (Cheryl) saw that the class list included people from Taiwan, mainland China, and Hong Kong. From previous experience, I knew that those collective identities may be defined with clear in- and out-groups based on historical events and definitions of nationality within each region. However, I did want to give them a choice to create a new in-group by being in the class. As a result, I was careful not to ask people to represent their culture or country of origin; instead, I focused on personal experiences so they could get to know each other through sharing on more comfortable topics. After this trust was built, students could choose to share some of their collective stories if they wished. A few did and we were able to listen carefully to opposing versions of history and contemporary events without defensiveness or animosity from the students on the other side. We even came to a realization that we might never resolve the differing stories, but that our connection in the classroom together was a new story we could tell.

PERSONAL IDENTITIES

When thinking of reconciliation on a smaller scale, personal identity becomes even more important than our collective identities. While we carry our collective identities with us, each of us carries these differently, and this is where possibilities for change exist. My people may hate your people, but you and I can get along. This may not change whole systems at a time, but it does change the interactions between two individuals into an opportunity for peace and possibly reconciliation. This was demonstrated clearly in one English class designed for North and South Korean young adults to learn peacebuilding skills. The students from the North came from a unique situation as people who had left their homes to escape to the South, which had often been described to them as a promised land. The group from the South were made up of various learners, including office workers in mainstream society, staff from non-profit organizations, theology students, visiting international students from Japan, and even some young people with peace work experience. Although the students from South Korea had clear stereotypes about people from North Korea, their encounter with the young adults who had come from the North gave a first-hand, real-life experience that trumped all the propaganda and stories they had heard. Likewise, the students from the North learned of the complexity of society in the South from the unique perspectives of the diverse young people learning with them. For both groups, it was a transformative experience rooted in the personal and collective identities of the learners.

Of course, culture is not the only aspect of personal identity. Age, gender, abilities, family position, educational experience, profession, learning preferences, and personality characteristics will vary from student to student even if they hold collective identities in common. All of these variables will affect students' language learning and their interactions in the classroom, as well as their understandings of peace and how they work towards reconciliation. I (Jan) once taught an English class in Indonesia comprised of several Christian twenty-something men in seminary, two young sisters who were seamstresses and who were devout

Muslims, an older man who did carpentry odd jobs and who was a secular Muslim, and an older Chinese businesswoman. Though all were Indonesian, the other identities of the students made for an extremely diverse classroom!

IDENTITIES INTERACTING IN THE CLASSROOM

Not only do learners bring their own unique, dynamic identities into the classroom, each of these individuals interacts in unique ways in the group. The way students position themselves and others in the class relies greatly on their collective and personal identities. Who are the leaders in the class? Who are the quiet ones? Which small groups work well together? Which obviously struggle when paired up? Whose voices are the loudest in the class? What patterns of behavior, communication, and learning do they establish for other students? All of these questions relate to the group dynamics.

ELEMENTS OF GROUP DYNAMICS

When individuals come together to form a group, an interesting process occurs. This phenomenon of group formation has been studied by researchers in sociology, and there are different theories as to what happens. One influential theory suggests that there are four main stages of group development (Tuckman and Jensen 1977). First, the group is in the "forming" stage which allows people to get to know each other on the surface. In diverse groups, this can take a while because group members do not share as many experiences in common. The second stage is "storming." It is generally a more uncomfortable stage during which group members voice their opinions and become more real with one another, sometimes resulting in conflict or at least some disagreements. The third stage is "norming." In this stage, the group starts to follow certain patterns of behavior. These patterns may be deliberate, but they will most likely just emerge from the interactions of the group. The "norms" that result are powerful boundaries on what the group members may or may not do; however, this level of cohesion allows the group to function well together.

The next stage is "performing" in which the group has a deeper level of trust and understanding with one another and the way they work together, which allows them to perform to their best abilities. The group's energy can focus on the task at hand rather than on each other or conflicts in the group because there is clear yet flexible structure that supports group members in their tasks.

Of course, this is only one theory and in reality, groups do not always move through clear stages in a linear order. Critics of this theory note that intercultural groups in particular may not follow such linear group development and may have to work harder at communication during all the stages. However, this terminology can be a helpful starting place for English language teachers to recognize ways that groups develop and to watch for shifting dynamics at different times during group work or in the class as a whole.

Another key concept in working with group dynamics is power. The term "power" can mean many different things depending on context. What does it mean in the language classroom? First, it is important to recognize that everyone has some sort of power because power exists between people and is not a finite resource. In relationship, though, power can appear in different ways. One person can have power upon (exploitation), over (manipulation), against (competition), for (empowerment), or with (collaboration) someone else. Each of these kinds of power can be present in relationships between learners in educational settings. They are not mutually exclusive, but rather fluid and changing through their interactions. How we work with learners in groups helps us to recognize and move away from more exploitative kinds of power, which are often harmful, and towards more collaborative kinds of power, which can work to heal harms and enable reconciliation.

FIG. 2: SOURCES AND DOMAINS OF POWER

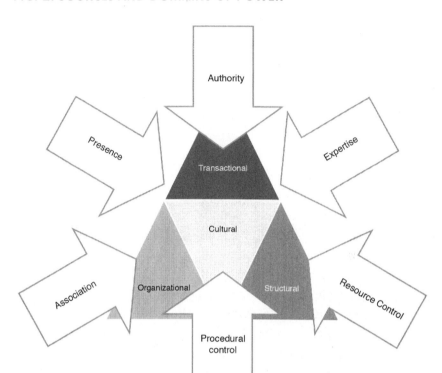

There are also different sources of power that are helpful to recognize in group work. Power can be understood to come from needing others to reach our goals, which means that power in a relationship depends on what one person needs and what the other person possesses (Armster and Amstutz 2008). The arrows in Figure 2 show a few of these sources of power. For example, if you have information or personal *associations* that I need, you will have power in our relationship. Likewise, if you have *resource* or *procedural control* that will help me reach my goal, you will have power. You may have a charismatic *presence* or be in a role of *authority* that can also be a source of power. Knowing about these sources of power can help teachers design group work that addresses any imbalances of power among members. For example, giving each person specific information or tasks in group work

(See the "Group Duties" task in Appendix A) or including students in designing and facilitating group procedures can help empower all group members.

In addition to kinds and sources of power, we can think of different domains of power, as shown by the triangles in Figure 2. Power can be found in our interpersonal interactions (*transactional domain*), in the formal or informal agreements that we support (*organizational domain*), or in the frameworks of how we arrange our roles and responsibilities (*structural domain*) (Armster and Amstutz 2008). These domains interact dynamically in the classroom and affect how students relate to each other in groups. For example, two students in the same group may find it difficult to work together if one student tries to exert power over the other student on the transactional domain by repeatedly interrupting and dismissing the other student's ideas. Other students in the group might contribute to the problem if they agree that the dominating student is the leader and follow along on the organizational domain. If the dominating student is male or older than the other students, there may be structural elements of power at play. Working to change power dynamics from all of these domains might be difficult, but sometimes just addressing one domain can open up space for new interactions in the group. For instance, a teacher who sees this happening can intervene to set up new contractual agreements, such as making sure everyone gets a chance to speak (See "Speech Equalizer" in Appendix A) or writing ideas down before sharing them verbally.

A final domain of power is rooted in our identities through the stories we tell and the metaphors we use (*cultural domain*). We often value certain kinds of stories and knowledge more than others based on our own assumptions, which can result in viewing these ways of knowing as more powerful than others. This happens in the classroom, for example, when group members "report back" from a group discussion and the speaker on behalf of the group mentions only certain stories that were shared or reframes them in a different way. Teachers can work in the cultural domain by paying attention to which stories they value from students. Is there a "right" answer to the question? If so, for whom is it right? Which narratives are privileged? Is there space to negotiate, validate, and value multiple meanings (Woelk 2015)? Language teachers have a unique opportunity to learn about power imbalances on the cultural domain by listening to student voices in group work and hearing which worldviews and ways of knowing are valued over others while reflecting on their own assumptions. In working for reconciliation, teachers can also help students to become aware of these power dynamics and possibly reshape some of our assumptions and our worldviews.

A final element of groups which is helpful for language teachers to keep in mind is the dynamic of mainstreams and margins. This is the idea that in any group of people, a subgroup often emerges as the dominant mainstream, and members who differ from the dominant subgroup become marginalized (Lakey 2010). This is not necessarily an intentional effort on behalf of the mainstream group to exclude certain people (although it can be), but rather a result of the group members searching for common ground in order to form norms and patterns that members can follow in order to complete their tasks successfully. Despite good intentions, however, the resulting marginalization experienced by those whose voices differ from the mainstream can be a source of conflict in the group. Even if conflict does not arise, the division between mainstream and margins limits the diversity of ideas that the group might need to get the job done. When this limiting is extreme, groups can succumb to "group-think," which is essentially when a group is stuck in thinking only one way about a problem rather than trying multiple, creative approaches. Thankfully, the dynamic of mainstream and margins can be transformed when the group becomes aware of their reality and makes space for voices that have been excluded from the conversation. Teachers can be facilitators of this awareness in the group and create protocols to limit the marginalization of different perspectives. Including marginalized voices can add greatly to the group's success and also bring about opportunities for reconciliation in times of conflict.

Given all these factors of group dynamics, it's easy to see how a class may set up their own unique patterns of interaction different from any other. Upon reflection, I (Cheryl) can see now that the differences in my two fall classes had a lot to do with different group formation and norms. The first class was one cohesive group, in which students seemed to intentionally bring in those on the margins. The second class had a clear mainstream group that didn't make many attempts to include students on the margins, although some students seemed content with disengaging a bit from interactive group work and preferred individual tasks. In the first class' group development, norms appeared that kept pair and group work going beyond my instructions, prompting rich dialogue and questioning. In the second class, students only completed the instructions as given and then passively waited for more. As a whole class, however, they asked more questions, sometimes challenging the teacher. As a result, I enjoyed the first class a little more, but the second class probably got more information and detailed instruction from me. By the end of the term, students in both classes successfully achieved their learning objectives and gave fairly similar evaluations on their feedback at the end of the term. They were both "good" classes, but very different.

OPPORTUNITIES FOR NEW INTERACTIONS

The language classroom, then, can become a place to make new in-groups and redefine interactions. A first step in accomplishing this goal is getting to know learner identities through eliciting information from students themselves as they feel comfortable, allowing students to define themselves by the categories you set instead of someone else defining them. It's important to avoid asking one person to speak on behalf of their culture or in-group as defined by someone else. We can prompt learners to reflect on what they want to share and how they share it, while making space for them to articulate their own stories if they choose. Valuing our students' experiences, whether they are children or adults, can be transformative. What learners present in the classroom is a small piece of their lives, which are rich, complex, and storied. Showing we are interested and that we care about more than just their test results can set the stage for transformation. Building relationships takes time, but the classroom can often provide ideal settings where this can occur.

One type of opportunity for new interactions in the classroom is through group work. It is sometimes tempting, as the teacher, to use group-work time as a chance to think about what comes next in class or take a break and tune out for a minute. In working for peacebuilding in the classroom, though, this is possibly the most important time to pay attention. Watching student interaction can help teachers to prevent and deal with conflicts that arise and maximize opportunities for learning and developing transformative relationships. It's helpful to experiment with groupings and monitor how they go. What can teachers watch for as they're monitoring? We can pay attention to the level of engagement in the task, the amount of talk happening, the balance of talk time among group members, the facial expressions and body language of group members that may indicate enthusiasm or frustration, and the distribution of duties or tasks in the group. It's also helpful to watch for how group members interact after the group work has ended. Do they eagerly move back to their seats or do they continue their conversation beyond the required tasks? This monitoring can help teachers to see whether certain identities in the class are interacting in positive or potentially harmful ways. All of these can point to power imbalances or patterns of exclusion that a teacher can help learners to recognize and counter in order to move toward creating a space for reconciliation.

In addition to opportunities for new interactions on personal and group levels, we can help create a different kind of whole group experience in the class. Usually, it is fairly easy to notice who is in the mainstream and who is on the margins in a class. These dynamics happen often by the end of the first class together. One of the first things that people wonder when being part of a group is who are these people and who am I in relationship to them? The answers to these questions help people decide whether they will take on leadership roles and speak up or whether they will observe and hold back; whether they feel safe to be themselves or whether they need to guard against possible harm. It is important for teachers to be aware of those individuals who end up on the margins as those in the mainstream may not notice this dynamic. Teachers can simply draw awareness to voices that have not been heard by asking to hear from someone who has not spoken yet or by highlighting comments from the margins to the group. At times, it may be appropriate to be even more deliberate in helping the class notice the dynamics, not as a criticism, but as a strategy for learning from diverse perspectives. Drawing our students' attention to the classroom dynamics can help our students broaden their awareness of other identities in the room and may change the ways in which they interact with others to include multiple perspectives.

Finally, it is essential that teachers working for reconciliation create opportunities for new interactions in response to conflict in the classroom. Conflict is normal and can even be an opportunity to grow closer to one another or to function better as a group. Although it is natural to tend to avoid any conflict, there is really no need to fear it. The more often we practice facing conflict and working for collaborative solutions to problems together, the more we will find practices and strategies to help us work through conflict. Responding in healthy ways to conflict starts with noticing interactional dynamics and seeking to intervene before conversations get too heated. Consciously monitoring all the dynamics and interactions in the classroom is not easy and takes a lot of practice and intention to learn. This learning can begin by teachers paying attention to their own feelings during the class. A teacher's feelings often reflect students' feelings or point to of aspects of identity that need attention in this context.

For example, I (Cheryl) taught a class in which there was one man who was quite engaged and vocal. Every time he spoke, he had great questions that involved a lot of discussion and explanation, and he took leadership in all the activities that we did. He seemed like a nice, likeable guy. Over the course of the term, however, I found myself getting more and more irritated with his interruptions and way of communicating. At times, I was even feeling angry, and I found myself thinking of him outside of the class, reliving different incidents with him from the day. I could not understand why this was becoming a point of frustration for me. Eventually, I realized that these feelings of mine were a reflection of feelings of some of those on the margins in the group. I started watching a few people in the class who were not as enthusiastic about his leadership and how they responded when he interrupted with one of his excellent questions. I realized that there was a level of frustration in the group because not everyone wanted to go in the direction he was heading. He was taking up a lot of class time, leaving little room for other identities to interact fully. In the end, I made an effort to shift the dynamics with the group by trying to redirect some of his questions to private conversations after class.

Once conflict emerges, we can still create opportunities for interacting in new ways. This can include trying to do what we can to indirectly shift the dynamics of the classroom. Perhaps grouping students differently or changing an activity can be enough to allow students to work out their conflicts. Sometimes, though, more direct intervention is necessary. Facilitated dialogue or even mediation can be a way to help students move through the conflict to a place where they can work together again (see Armster and Amstutz 2008 for materials related to facilitating these processes). With the academic research and writing class described in chapter 1, in which group work failed due to problems that arose and the lack of conflict resolution skills of group members, I had asked for advice from colleagues on how to handle this. Suggestions included "Be strict! Give them an 'F' so they get their act together!" or "Break them up and add each of them to the other groups so they can get things done." I did not feel good about either of these options. Instead I decided to meet directly with each of the group members to talk about what was going on and ask if they would be willing to engage in a conflict resolution process. After some discussion on both sides, we eventually met together for a mediation session during which the group realized how their communication had impacted other group members and how cultural understandings played a big part in their conflict. The learners were able to reconcile for the purpose of the project and, in the end, came out with an exemplary collaborative essay and presentation that inspired the rest of the class.

Often teachers try to manage classroom dynamics all on their own, but in reality, everyone has conflict resolution skills that they can contribute. Relying on learners' abilities to work through conflicts, particularly in intercultural settings, can sometimes be more effective than any mediation attempts we as teachers might make. For instance, in a university-level intensive English program in the United States, there was a situation where two Saudi students came to blows during class over an incident that administrators could not quite understand. As the administration team debated how to deal with the situation and what might be appropriate consequences from a university perspective, the idea came up to ask several mature students in the Saudi student community what cultural practices they had for dealing with a conflict. As it turned out, one of the best approaches was for other community members to get involved. A classroom was set aside for the group to meet together and deal with the conflict in Arabic in the way that they saw fit. After they were finished, they reported what the students promised to do to make it up to the teacher and other students in the class and what they would do to avoid another conflict. Inviting the students to be part of the decision-making was far more successful than any approach the school leadership could have devised!

When we consider learner identities in all their complexity and make space for their identities to be present, to grow, and to change together, language learning becomes an opportunity for relating to others in new ways that can lead to reconciliation.

PRACTICAL APPLICATION—NURTURING AWARENESS OF LEARNER IDENTITIES

(Note: All activities mentioned are described in Appendix A.)
1. *Keep the demographics in mind and ask open-ended questions.* Gather as much information about students as possible before class begins. Plan time for eliciting information from the

students themselves through introduction exercises that allow students to define themselves according to categories you set. Activities such as "Group-up" or "Total Physical Response Warm-up" can be effective.

2. *Get to know each student as an individual.* Make an effort to learn each student's name and how to pronounce it correctly, on the very first day. Ask them what they would like to be called rather than making an assumption about nicknames, given names, or adopted English names. Use a task like "I Am From . . . Poems" to allow students to share about themselves. If you find it difficult to remember details or if you have many students, keep a "cheat sheet" with notes about students beyond their basic information that are helpful for you to know who they are. Review your notes before planning lessons or before class.

3. *Watch group and pair work closely.* Monitor group work and take notes on how groups or pairs work together. Plan groupings intentionally, keeping in mind identities and power issues that you have noticed in the class. Have some activities in which groups and pairs change frequently, such as "Concentric Circles" and have other tasks in which students always meet with the same person, such as "Vocabulary Partners," to give students both variety and security. Watch groups as they work together and look for any signs of power imbalances or potential areas of conflict. Notice what stages of group development students are in, so you will be prepared to coach them in their work.

4. *Be intentional about working with mainstreams and margins.* Find ways to draw in those from the margins through different types of class activities, such as "Group Duties" or "Card Sorts." Depending on the class, it may be helpful to talk more overtly about group dynamics through tasks such as "Mainstreams and Margins" or to provide opportunities for experiential learning with any language level, or even younger learners, in an exercise such as "More and Less."

5. *Notice your feelings as flags of potential conflict.* Pay attention to how you are feeling during class and while watching students interact. Practice checking in with yourself before

wrapping up group or pair work tasks to check if you might be sensing any discomfort that is present in the room. If you find yourself thinking about a particular student or incident between learners, reflect on it further. How might each learner's identity play a role in this incident? What struggles might learners be facing in terms of identity formation? How might in- and out-groups play a role? What potential for further conflict might exist? Brainstorm ways to address the issues you have identified either indirectly or directly, depending on the context. Discuss your ideas with colleagues if possible.

6. *Plan for conflict and view it as potential for learning and growth.* Given the reality of our learners and classrooms, conflicts will likely happen at some point. Depending on the language proficiency level of the class, teachers may wish to talk about how to communicate when problems arise in the group. Decide how and when you will intervene, beginning by giving group members agency in deciding how they will respond to the conflict, but also having a back-up plan for intervention if needed.

CONCLUSION

Understanding, valuing, and using learner identity as an asset in the language classroom is complex and multifaceted work. Every group is unique and dynamic, and there are no clear-cut ways to handle conflicts that arise. Like Cheryl's two classes discussed at the beginning of this chapter, differences in identity can directly shape classroom experiences and how we need to respond to create opportunities for peacebuilding or reconciliation. When working for reconciliation in the classroom, any effort that Christian English language teachers make to pay attention to the identities of the learners and how they interact will be valuable in creating a more peaceful space that can allow for new ways of interaction and transformation of our identities.

CHAPTER 6

TEACHERS

INTRODUCTION

I (Jan) am frequently asked for suggestions of materials or curriculum to use in English classes, especially by those in ministry contexts. Often the conversation goes something like this one, with a fictitious participant named "Sue":

> **Sue:** I'm teaching English in Colombia, and I wondered if you have any ideas for good materials.
> **Jan:** Okay, well, what are the students' goals and needs?
> **Sue:** They want to learn English.
> **Jan:** Do you know what they need English for?
> **Sue:** Everyone in Colombia wants to learn English!
> **Jan:** Okay, let's try a different topic . . . what are their English levels?
> **Sue:** What do you mean? They know some English.
> **Jan:** Hmmm . . . well, what methods are you using?
> **Sue:** I'm using a book. But I don't think it's the best book for the students, so I wonder what you would suggest.

While I am sympathetic to Sue's request, I think to myself that what Sue *most* needs is not a better book, but some training in teaching English. A great many people find themselves inadvertently teaching English in mission or church programs. It was not something they had prepared for, but they reason that if they can just get the right materials, all will be well. (We *do* talk about materials in the next section of this book, and we hope that this book may provide some helpful background and guidance for those who find themselves teaching English, even though they are untrained.)

However, "materials" are not the pivotal key ingredient in the language classroom. That distinction goes to the *teacher*. It is the teacher who has the potential to inspire and motivate. It is the teacher who can choose methods which will be effective in helping the learners reach their goals. It is the teacher who opens up space in the classroom for students to grow and achieve their God-given potential. And it is the teacher who can set the tone and lay the groundwork for reconciliation and peacebuilding to happen within an English class. Materials are optional; a good teacher is not.

Before we move into a discussion of the teacher's role in the classroom, however, it is important to address the issue of teacher identity. Just as learners all bring their unique identities into the classroom space as described in the previous chapter, teachers also transform and are transformed by others based on the identities brought into the mix. Learning about our own identities and positioning in relation to students and colleagues is the first step to working for reconciliation. This learning includes recognizing the power that comes with the role of teacher. Teachers will never be on the same power level as students, no matter how much they succeed at learner-centered practices and empowering students. When teachers recognize the power dynamic that is part of their relationship with the students, and thus a salient part of their identity in the classroom, there is actually more freedom for teachers to be intentional in how they interact and for students to be empowered and utilize their power in the class. Many aspects of the teacher's identity such as gender, age, ethnic background, nationality, religion, and other factors can also be viewed in light of power balances and can greatly affect how students perceive teachers, thus influencing how students learn. Are teachers clearly in the "out-group"? Or are there connections that help students and teachers relate? Being aware of one's own identity and how it affects the class is an important part of creating a space for building peace and reconciliation.

In this chapter, we will explore the critical role of the teacher in creating classroom experiences which foster reconciliation. First, we will introduce the concept of the "hidden curriculum." Then we will look at two areas of the classroom over which the teacher has control: 1) one's own *dispositions,* or character qualities, and 2) the choice of methods. We will see how these impact, or more accurately even *determine,* whether and how reconciliation can flourish in the classroom.

THE HIDDEN CURRICULUM

Most people are familiar with the concept of a "curriculum" as the content to be covered in a course of study. There is nothing hidden about this type of curriculum. Teacher's guides, charts of objectives, and learner textbooks usually take center stage in the teaching and learning process. When there is a good curriculum, everyone knows what material is to be taught, and everyone assumes that this same material will be learned.

But often what is taught is *not* learned. And sometimes what is actually learned in the classroom is not something that has been taught. This is where the hidden curriculum comes in. Michael Haralambos (1991) has defined the *hidden curriculum* as "those things pupils learn through the experience of attending school rather than the stated educational objectives of such institutions" (p. 1). It is anything that students learn in the classroom that was not overtly taught. It is what students "pick up" from what takes place in the classroom.

For example, the hidden curriculum in many classrooms includes the belief that "Students should be silent." There is probably no written curriculum explicitly stating, "Teach students to be quiet." And yet the messages which subtly or not so subtly teach students to be silent are abundant: "Everyone be quiet!"; "Listen to the teacher"; "Raise your hand before you speak." Students quickly learn that the classroom is no place for conversation.

As another example, consider a perspective on errors. Teachers may claim that they want students to feel free to make mistakes, but the hidden curriculum in their classrooms may suggest otherwise.

If student responses are met with praise when correct but disapproval when incorrect, students quickly learn not to speak up unless they are certain their answer is correct. This suppression of risk-taking and trial and error is quite damaging for language learners—in fact for all learners.

But the hidden curriculum does not need to be negative. Students could also be developing respect for others, excitement about learning, and hopefulness for their futures. They might be learning that their opinions have value, that sarcasm is counterproductive in honest dialogue, and that it is good to ask questions before jumping to conclusions. Can you see where this is going? What tremendous opportunities we have to build reconciliatory skills through intentional consideration of our hidden curriculum!

CHARACTER

A teacher's character plays a significant role in determining what hidden curriculum students experience in the classroom. What do students learn from the teacher's attitudes about languages and cultures? What do they learn from the teacher's joyfulness or lack thereof about purpose and fulfillment in life? What do they learn from their interactions with the teacher about relationships? We will look at teacher character through two lenses: teacher *dispositions,* and the *fruit of the spirit.*

TEACHER DISPOSITIONS

In the 1990s educators began to talk about the "dispositions" needed by teachers. This was apparently an effort to place performance values on "attitudes" (Freeman 2007), and within just a few years NCATE (National Council for Accreditation of Teacher Education)[3] had adopted dispositional requirements for teacher certification. According to CAEP, teacher dispositions are "The habits of professional action and moral commitments that underlie an educator's performance" (CAEP Glossary, p. 8). I (Jan) began to

---

[3] NCATE merged into CAEP, the Council for the Accreditation of Educator Preparation, an American teacher education accrediting body.

take an earnest look at dispositions a few years ago, in an effort to raise my teacher trainees' awareness of the dispositions that I felt were essential in TESOL. I identified six dispositions that I wanted students to actively cultivate as future English teachers. These are:

EMPATHY—Teachers should show compassion for ELLs (English Language Learners) facing a difficult, complex, humbling, frustrating, personal, and often lonely language-learning task.

EQUALITY—Teachers should understand that other cultural perspectives, languages, places, and systems are enjoyed by their people and are meaningful and effective. We should not think of one culture, language, or country as "better" than others.

EXPECTATION—Teachers should maintain high standards for learner achievement based on the understanding that ELLs are capable of learning English to a high level and have the right to accomplish their learning within a reasonable time frame.

EQUITY—Teachers should provide each student with what he or she needs, knowing that needs will differ and may require different learning experiences for different students.

ENJOYMENT—Teachers should bear the responsibility for making class time interesting, challenging, effective, positive, and enjoyable.

EMPOWERMENT—Teachers should facilitate a path for students towards a point where ELLs can become autonomous learners.

How might these dispositions be instrumental in a teacher's efforts to build reconciliation into an English learning classroom?

Empathy: This is the ability to put oneself in another's shoes. Empathy is a prerequisite for peacebuilding. As the teacher models empathy, students are more likely to develop it as well.

Equality: The teacher demonstrates the perspective that different languages and cultures have equal value. This equal footing is needed for respectful dialogue. Note that this does not mean that all elements of all cultures are good. Just as an individual's characteristics are complex (good, flawed, and changing), cultures are systems made up of these complex people, so they are always shifting and changing. Equality is about taking away a judgement attached to the discussion of culture and instead making space for discussion of these complexities.

Expectation: The teacher expects great and life-altering things to happen in the classroom, in English learning and relationship building, and this wondrous sense of expectation rubs off on the students. They care more and invest more in classroom experiences. Students quickly learn that the English classroom is not just a place to learn about nouns and verbs, but it is a place to relate and grow as human beings.

Equity: The teacher demonstrates equity by meeting individual student needs. Students learn that people are different, and that "fairness" is not necessarily "sameness." Teachers who strive for equity in the language-learning classroom pay close attention to the student identities discussed in chapter 5, and to students' individual language-learning needs. The lens of "equity" frees teachers to individualize learning experiences so that each student receives what he or she needs in the classroom.

Enjoyment: Many English learners around the world have seldom had the delight of enjoyable classes, and would even find it odd that "enjoyment" could be expected in an English class! Students spend long hours memorizing grammar rules, filling in worksheets, and working through difficult and uninspiring texts with the help of a dictionary—activities which are not inherently enjoyable for the majority of learners. As a teacher injects joy into daily classroom experiences through his or her demeanor, student stress and defensiveness is lowered, opening the door for meaningful, non-threatening dialogue.

Empowerment: A teacher's greatest dispositional ally in working for reconciliation may lie in the ability to empower the learners. Students can be challenged to take ownership of their learning, relationships, and lives within the context of an English classroom.

Of course, other dispositions that would have a positive impact on reconciliatory goals in the English language classroom could also be identified. We could add words such as *honesty* and *persistence* to the list, for example. We would encourage you to come up with a list of dispositions that you believe can be helpful in building bridges and fostering good relationships in your own context, and then actively seek to cultivate and demonstrate those. You may want to create a weekly self-checking system so that you are continually asking yourself how well you are modeling the targeted dispositions for your students.

FRUIT OF THE SPIRIT

As Christians, we do not have to just rely on intuition or handed-down wisdom to know what qualities should be on display in our lives. We have been given God's Word and the perfect teacher model in the life of Jesus Christ. A full discussion on what it means to be "Christian" in all aspects of our teaching lives is beyond the scope of this book. However, as we are talking about teacher character, one passage is especially relevant: "The fruit of the Spirit is love, joy, peace, patience, kindness, goodness, faithfulness, gentleness, self-control. . ." (Gal 5:22–23, ESV).

You will probably readily agree that a teacher who demonstrates these nine character qualities is certainly modeling the qualities needed for peacebuilding. In fact, the number one statement about teachers who have had a lasting impact on their students is usually something like "He/she really cared about me." Loving and showing kindness to students always has the most impact on their lives. Of course, one way we do this is through excellence in teaching. But our care and compassion for our students should go beyond teaching effectiveness and permeate our relationships with them. So, our need to love our students and show kindness to them in the classroom is a given. Our need to be joyful has already been addressed above. But there are three remaining fruits in this passage which impact our goals of reconciliation in the classroom: peace, patience, and self-control.

Classrooms are normally *peaceful*. Though sometimes students misbehave or do not pay attention when they should, fistfights are rare, and classrooms around the world are characterized by students sitting quietly in their seats listening to the teacher. But just because the atmosphere is peaceful, does that mean there is *peace*? No. It just means everyone has accepted the hidden curriculum demanding that students be silent. In any given student group, there are probably those who don't like each other, but because they do not interact in the classroom, the illusion of peace is maintained. What if, instead of having a goal of "peacefulness," we actually had a goal of *peace?* Then, the classroom might look and sound very different. There might be loud exchanges as people take the opportunity to say what they really think. There might be uncomfortable feelings, and *peace* may not emerge within a standard fifty-five-minute class period, but the ultimate outcome over the course of a semester or year could be greatly increased *peace* among learners.

To exemplify such a pursuit of peace over peacefulness, imagine a group of teenagers in an inner-city ESL class. The Hispanic boys have been making fun of the Sikh boys in the hallway, ridiculing their turbans. This animosity has never erupted in the classroom, as students normally sit passively while completing ESL worksheets. Today, however, the ESL teacher has decided to embrace the potential for reconciliation in the classroom and has prepared an activity that she hopes will develop empathy and begin to build bridges between the two groups. Students will work together in pairs to discover similarities and differences in how they demonstrate respect in their homes. The teacher pairs Hispanic and Sikh students together and doesn't back down when the expected moans and objections initially cause a dark cloud of hostility to settle over the classroom. The teacher listens as students reluctantly begin to share with their partners. A Hispanic student says, "I work in store after the school . . . bring money. This my respect." Then from the Sikh partner, "I wear turban because my dad . . . very angry if I do not wear it!" The Hispanic student challenges this perspective: "Why you not take off [turban] in school? You dad . . . he not see you." The Sikh boy at first seems to cower in silence, but then finds the courage to come back quietly with, "That is no respect. You only respect if your dad here? Respect mean all times. You only work if your dad there?" Silence ensues. The boys are far from friendship. But whether they realize it or not, they have begun to build bridges. They are talking—and talking about things that matter. Through many more such activities, true *peace* can be built, by giving up temporary *peacefulness.* Even if students are at lower English levels and cannot engage in complex dialogue, they can benefit from being paired together to share experiences and tasks. Just working alongside one another can often begin to increase understanding and melt animosity.

In order to continue to engage students in lessons like the one above, this teacher will need an abundance of *patience* and *self-control,* the remaining fruits of the spirit. Long-standing animosities do not disappear overnight. Real relationships are not like the movies where arch enemies become good friends in the two hours it takes to eat a bowl of popcorn. Instead, when classroom experiences include purposeful relationship-building, students can seem at first to become more defensive than ever. Patience is certainly needed in order to keep this pursuit a priority for the duration of the course or program.

And what about *self-control?* What does that look like in the context of reconciliatory goals? Perhaps one face of it is the ability to "let go and let God." We can plan the lessons and set the plan in motion in the classroom. We can also sometimes act as facilitators as we pose thoughtful questions or elicit more dialogue. But much of what happens in the classroom is up to the students and the working of the Holy Spirit in their lives. More than once I have resorted to imagining a piece of duct tape over my mouth to make sure that I did not insert myself into conversations where I had no business being. Of course, there is a time to step in if dialogue becomes hurtful or derogatory. But reconciliation is messy business, and our tendency as teachers to want to make everything go smoothly can sometimes get in the way.

METHODOLOGY

While half of a teacher's job involves *being*—demonstrating the dispositions and fruit of the Spirit which can help others learn and grow—the other half involves planning for learning and carrying out those plans. The plans that we have for instruction are typically encoded in *methodology*—what students and teachers do in the classroom. We address methodology in more detail in chapter 7. Here, we want to discuss characteristics of the activities that teachers choose for class engagement. We introduce the acronym REAL (see Fig. 3) as a template for selecting activities which can foster bridge-building and reconciliation.

FIG. 3: REAL ACTIVITIES IN TEACHING ENGLISH FOR RECONCILIATION

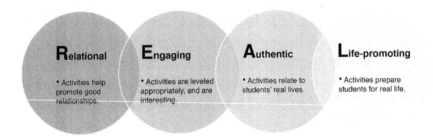

Relational
• Activities help promote good relationships.

Engaging
• Activities are leveled appropriately, and are interesting.

Authentic
• Activities relate to students' real lives.

Life-promoting
• Activities prepare students for real life.

Each of these qualities will be discussed here, and then in chapter 7 specific methods will be introduced which meet the REAL criteria.

RELATIONAL

Many language classes are characterized by students sitting at desks with their noses in their books. While there are times when textbooks are helpful, sometimes textbooks do not do a great job of facilitating relationships. Imagine that the topic of a lesson is family words, and students are looking at the family tree of "Pedro" in a textbook, making sentences about his family members. There's just one problem: Pedro is not real. His family is not real. There is no relationship-building happening through this activity. Contrast this with a scenario in which the teacher has given students a blank template of her own family tree. The students have the names of her family members on small squares of paper, and must ask the teacher questions in order to discover where the names belong on the family tree. Students are practicing question word order as they ask questions like "Who is Max?" and possessives as they ask questions such as "Who is Nathan's sister?" This activity is building relationships between the teacher and her students! Later, the students will create blank templates and name cards of their own family trees, and repeat the activity with each other. They will learn about each other's families, and relationships will grow.

Relational methods can be as simple as a thirty-second verbal exchange in which students share something about their lives with a classmate or more complex like the family tree task. Students can be sharing fun facts about themselves, such as their favorite flavor of ice cream, or deeper personal information, such as their greatest fear or most important life goal. The filtering question to ask is this: Are we talking about the people in the room? If so, it is probably a relationship-building activity. If the conversation is about fictional characters in books, it may not be.

ENGAGING

Little of value happens in a classroom where students are either passive or altogether tuned out. An engaging class, in contrast, is one in which students are actively involved in using language. We know that engagement is necessary for language acquisition. People learn language by using language—by reading, writing, speaking, and listening for meaningful communication. And engagement is also necessary in order for the classroom to be a place of transformation and growth.

Consider a language classroom in Indonesia where high beginning-level students are starting to learn past tense forms. A passive, unengaging, and uninspired lesson might consist of the teacher writing the rule for past tense formation on the board, illustrating how we add "ed" to regular verbs to make past forms. The teacher might then hand out a worksheet on which students change present verbs to past. I am almost put to sleep even writing about such a class. Imagine instead a teacher committed to making every class student-centered and engaging. This teacher begins by talking about a funny thing that happened to her on the weekend. She tells students this story:

> On Saturday morning, I wanted coffee. I filled the coffee maker with water. When I poured in the water, a lizard popped out! I screamed! My husband asked what was wrong. I responded that I didn't want coffee any more.

Being aware of the students' low language level, she has brought a coffeemaker, water, and toy lizard to class, to demonstrate what happened. She then gives students a printed copy of the story. She says, "Underline *ed*." She demonstrates on the board by writing the word "wanted," and underlining "ed." She then asks students to work in small groups to write a rule about using "ed." She allows them to talk in their first language if needed. She asks students to come up to the board and write their rules. She provides feedback to elicit accurate statements. The class selects this one to write in their grammar notebooks: **Add "ed" to make past.** This is an engaging class. It begins with a personal story (talking about the people in the room), and concludes with an inductive learning task: discovering the rule from examples.

AUTHENTIC

"Authenticity" has become an important concept in English language teaching. There is talk of authentic language, authentic materials, and authentic tasks, all acknowledging that the language we teach our students should be the *real* language that they need for *real* communication. In order to be effective English teachers, then, we need to ensure authenticity in all of the language and language learning tasks that we set for our students.

For teachers desiring to open spaces for reconciliation in the language classroom, embracing authenticity can have a far-reaching impact on our methodology. As we encourage authentic language, for example, we may be challenged to teach language that does not normally appear in language course books, such as phrases used in asking for and offering forgiveness. To teach this kind of authentic language, consider the following chant:

Forgiveness Chant

I'm really very sorry; please forgive me!
    It's alright; that's okay ... Please don't worry about it.
I shouldn't have done that; I was wrong; please forgive me!
    It's alright; that's okay ... Please don't worry about it.
I'm sorry that I caused you pain; please forgive me!
    It's alright; that's okay ... Please don't worry about it.
I will try to do better next time; please forgive me!
    It's alright; that's okay ... Please don't worry about it.
Thank you, for understanding; thank you, for being kind.
    It's alright; that's okay ... You are ... forgiven!

We can also seek to use authentic materials. This commonly plays out in choices such as the use of real menus from local restaurants instead of textbook menus, and real grocery store products rather than simulated nutrition labels in a language book. We can extend this goal to other types of materials for the purposes of reconciliation. For example, students could read about a real local case of cyber-bullying and participate in discussions about the causes of and solutions to this problem. Or students could listen to an argument, identify how the speakers could be more respectful in their dialogue, and suggest ways that they could come to an agreement.

Finally, we can use authentic tasks. In English language teaching, authentic tasks are those which mirror real-world activities. For example, writing a letter is an authentic task because it is something people do in the real world. Making a phone call to a doctor's office would be another type of authentic, real-world task. As we look to embed authentic tasks for *reconciliation* into classroom experiences, the sky is the limit! Perhaps we design a role-play task, providing pairs of students with common scenarios where two people disagree about something. We may pre-teach some basic strategies and language for working through disagreements, then ask that students demonstrate what they have learned via the role-play. We could design an authentic marketing task, where one group of students needs to sell something to another group. What they may not realize is that marketing requires knowing the audience very well. As the authentic marketing task is carried out, students will learn things about each other that they never knew before, and a by-product of the activity may well be increased understanding of the perspectives of the "other."

No conversation on authenticity would be complete without making the point that we should live and breathe authenticity— both in and out of the classroom. As we live lives that are transparent, honest, and real, we model the authenticity that we hope will characterize our classrooms.

LIFE-PROMOTING

Many Christian teachers think of their methodology as being neutral. Methodology itself does not promote anything, they might say, but is just a vehicle for content. We would challenge this perspective, believing that the methodologies we choose can either foster or hinder the goals we have for student learning and growth, especially when considering a reconciliatory lens. To illustrate, let's return to the example of the two lessons on past tense given above. Why is the methodology in the first lesson, where the teacher explains and then students passively fill out a worksheet, less effective? Is it poor only because students are unlikely to develop as competent language users from such an activity? Or could there be a deeper moral or ethical problem with such lessons? We believe that the latter is true because schooling which puts the learner only in a passive and powerless role is not just ineffective—it is also deadening and wasteful of human potential.

Passivity in education can breed apathy and weaken the belief in one's own ability to discover, learn, and grow. Passive students believe that the teacher is the giver of all knowledge. This perspective is concerning in any content area, but it is especially damaging in language learning, as there is far too much language to be learned in the little class time that usually comprises a language course. Students who do not become active, autonomous learners will never achieve very high language levels. Our goal should be to select methods that *awaken* the desire to learn, not kill it.

While we always want students to be active language learners, our respect for cultural and contextual differences may sometimes mean that we need to choose more traditional methodologies than we would like. Certainly, a teacher who appears to ignore realities such as national tests and locally respected teaching practices in favor of her own "strange" methods may be in danger of burning rather than building bridges with schools, teachers, and students. Surely, as Christian teachers called to reconciliation, this is not our goal! However, we have experienced great openness in the global contexts in which we have taught the use of student-centered and autonomy-fostering methodologies. Teachers who approach new contexts with respect and humility, and who take the time to engage in dialogue about language learning goals and effective ways to reach those goals, will very likely experience gratitude for learner-focused methodologies that are REAL.

PRACTICAL APPLICATION:
BECOMING A RECONCILIATORY ENGLISH TEACHER

1. *Be aware of the hidden curriculum.* Cultivate a view of your classroom which continually asks, "What are students picking up in my classroom that I am not actively teaching them?
2. *Actively cultivate appropriate dispositions.* Make a list of dispositions that may most impact your teaching in your own context. The list in this chapter may serve as a useful starting point. Many teachers find it helpful to select one disposition at a time and pay special attention to it.

3. *Prayerfully consider whether the fruit of the spirit is evident in your classroom teaching.* For a period of time you may want to focus on one of the fruits each morning in your devotions. Ask yourself, "What can I do today to ensure that my students see this fruit in my life?"

4. *Begin looking at the selection of methods and activities for your classes through the REAL lens.* Consider adding the words "relational," "engaging," "authentic," and "life-promoting" at the top of each lesson plan. As you plan each activity, circle the words that you believe characterize the activity. If only one or two words are circled by the time you have finished preparing your plan, you may want to re-think some of your activities!

CONCLUSION

As a teacher, you will usually be the single most powerful force in the classroom. This is not because you possess great powers to change others, but rather because you will often be in a position to *empower* others—to open a space in which multiple voices may be heard. It is the teacher who can choose relationship-building and peacebuilding methodologies. And ultimately, it is the teacher who can purposefully allow the Holy Spirit to grow and display the fruits of the Spirit in his or her own life. The peacebuilding teacher is one who intentionally chooses these values and patterns in his or her life and classroom and teaches English for reconciliation.

PART 3

THE RESOURCES:
HOW CAN WE TEACH ENGLISH
FOR RECONCILIATION?

CHAPTER 7

CREATING CURRICULA FOR PEACE AND RECONCILIATION

INTRODUCTION

In the final section of this book we share practical ways to apply the framework introduced in the previous chapters, focused on relationships, issues, skills, methodology, and systems. In this chapter, we will look at ways to apply the framework in contexts where teachers have the freedom to choose their own topics, methods, and materials. In chapter 8 we will address contexts in which a curriculum, methods, and/or materials are fixed.

We begin by revisiting the story I (Jan) shared in the introduction to this book. This was a teaching context in which I had the freedom to select the topics, materials, and methods as I saw fit. To recap the situation, I had received a new group of adult immigrant English learners when teaching ESL in Ontario in the early 1990s. I had been aware of a war in far-off Yugoslavia, but did not consider the possibility that my new students might be refugees from that war. Perhaps someone should have told me that; nonetheless, I could have taken it upon myself to learn more about my new student group prior to meeting them, but did not. It simply did not occur to me to do this. So, even before stepping foot into the classroom on the first day, I failed in understanding the larger systems and issues which would affect my new class. At that time, as a new teacher, I understood planning for an ESL class only in terms of planning for language learning, so I had planned to give the students an assessment to find out their language levels and gather information about their professions and settlement needs. This information would guide me well, I thought, in developing language learning units on such practical topics as doctor's visits, meetings with their children's teachers, reading their rental contracts, and other life tasks. I failed to consider any emotional needs, animosities, culture shock, or conflicted identities stemming from the larger systems at play in the post-Yugoslavia context and era.

My concept of methodology was similarly restricted to language learning and teaching. I chose methodologies purely on the basis of the potential I felt they had for students to learn the language. I did not take into consideration, for example, whether or not students would *want* to work in pairs and with whom they might best work. I do not think it ever crossed my mind that an adult student might not want to pair with another student in the class, and if it had, I may well have blithely thought, "They are in Canada now; they need to get over their disagreements."

Finally, I was also limited in my understanding of the possible ramifications of issues and topics. Again, I thought of the topics utilized in class only in terms of language learning. For example, on that first day, the very first issue presented in class was the task of getting to know each other. I had not considered that this might not be the best topic for the first class, given where my students were coming from. I had planned to use a pair activity that I had used before. The task was to create a set of questions, based on the prompts I provided, and then to ask a partner these questions. When the group came back together, partners would introduce each other to the class. I thought of this task as rich with language learning potential. Students would demonstrate their awareness of question word order, practice speaking and listening during the interview, write notes, and then have an opportunity for more formal speaking in sharing with the whole class. The handout that students received looked something like this:

Learn about your new friend!
Discover these things about your friend:

Topic	Question	Answer
Home country		
First language		
Reason for coming to Canada		
Family members		
Profession		

Now, write a paragraph about your new friend!

Only years later did I think through how naïve and patronizing this worksheet may have appeared to those Yugoslav refugees. I now imagine that their unspoken reactions could have gone something like this:

Trigger phrase	Reaction
Friend	*Are you kidding me? MY people are never friends with THEIR people.*
Home country	*Don't you watch the news? I have no country.*
First language	*I don't want to say; others will label me*
Reason for coming to Canada	*I don't know how to say "death and destruction" in English.*
Family members	*Silence. Remembering family members killed or missing.*
Profession	*I know I will probably never have the English to work in my profession here, so who cares?*

My students clearly would have benefitted by having a teacher who understood, in terms of their potential for reconciliation, the systems, methodology, skills, issues, and relationships that are at play in a classroom. Not only had my students missed a chance for peacebuilding because I lacked this understanding, they also quite possibly were silenced even more, further entrenching the pain of the past rather than moving towards healing. So, what could I have done instead? In this chapter, we answer that question by working through the Reconciliatory English Teaching Framework (see Fig. 4). In Appendix B, a sample unit plan is given which could have been used in my class of Yugoslavian refugees. It incorporates many of the ideas in this chapter and could have provided a much more appropriate, reconciliation-focused series of classes for my students.

FIG. 4: RECONCILIATORY ENGLISH TEACHING FRAMEWORK

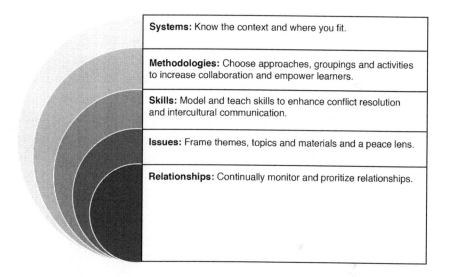

Systems: Know the context and where you fit.

Methodologies: Choose approaches, groupings and activities to increase collaboration and empower learners.

Skills: Model and teach skills to enhance conflict resolution and intercultural communication.

Issues: Frame themes, topics and materials and a peace lens.

Relationships: Continually monitor and prioritize relationships.

SYSTEMS: KNOW THE CONTEXT

Typically, English teachers think of planning in terms of meeting the stated course or lesson objectives. Teachers create unit and lesson plans to accomplish objectives such as "learning the parts of the body" or "making an invitation" or "writing a movie review." While planning for language learning is very important, we think there is yet a more basic level of planning that should come first: that which helps the teacher to understand the systems and contextual factors that will impact the teaching and learning environment.

What does it mean to understand the systems impacting English language learning and learners? Such understanding should include knowing as much as possible about both where students have come from and their current realities. For example, I certainly should have learned more about the Yugoslav war before the first day of my class. It would have helped considerably to know the factions, disputes, and outcomes of the war. I also needed to understand students' current realities. What were the conditions of their relocation to Canada? Were they living in communities alongside those with whom they had been at war? What resources were they being given to help in dealing with the traumas of war?

In addition to understanding these broader systems, contextual awareness involves knowing the particularities of student groups and individual students. Teachers typically do acquire some basic information about their students, such as their English language proficiency levels, what their native language is, and what additional languages they may speak. This is a good starting point. But there are many additional aspects of their identities which impact the learning context. For example, it is helpful to know not only what languages students know, but which ones are used for daily communication and with whom, which ones have been languages of academic instruction, and which ones are or are not developed to a high literacy level. Additional information to gather about students includes their personal and professional goals, jobs, family obligations, and resources such as internet or computers, transportation, and much more.

Finally, an understanding of larger systems and the learning context is incomplete without the teacher's own awareness of his or her identity and positionality within the given context. As discussed in chapter 6, teachers should approach a new teaching context from a position of self-reflection. In teaching the Yugoslavian student group, I never considered my own positionality within the Canadian government system, which sponsored refugees and paid for their English language learning. Yet I did act as an agent of that government system by delivering English language instruction, and that positionality affected student perceptions of me and my actions in the classroom.

In order to help teachers develop an awareness of the broader systems and contextual factors, we have created a tool entitled "Understanding a Teaching Context" in Appendix B. As a teacher works through the questions on this form, contextual understanding will increase, and teachers may become aware of larger systems impacting the teaching and learning environment. Building this understanding takes time and consideration, but it is an important first step in identifying the potential for peacebuilding and reconciliation within an English class.

METHODOLOGIES: CHOOSE APPROACHES, GROUPINGS, AND ACTIVITIES TO INCREASE COLLABORATION AND EMPOWER LEARNERS.

Methodology is one of the teacher's most powerful allies in teaching English for reconciliation. Methodology is central to the kind of learner-focused classroom that promotes second language acquisition, and it just so happens that many of these same methodologies are also instrumental in the pursuit of peacebuilding and conflict resolution. In this section, we will first discuss methodology as a broad, overarching *approach.* Then we will look at methodologies used in various classroom *groupings.* Finally, we will discuss specific *activities* that work well in teaching English for reconciliation. Throughout this section many sample activities are mentioned. Look for the full descriptions of activities in *italics* in Appendix A.

APPROACHES

An *approach* in language teaching can be thought of as the overarching way in which we intend to meet the stated course or program goals. The approach taken will determine what methods and materials are selected and how the learning will be assessed. As an example, let's look at the audiolingual approach, popularized in the seventies and still utilized in some places today. The goal underpinning this approach is that students should achieve correct pronunciation and automatic use of basic phrases by memorizing formulaic expressions and dialogues. This resulted in choosing activities in which students listened to dialogues, repeated them many times, and often commited them to memory. Though the emphasis on oral skills brought in by audiolingualism was a needed corrective to the earlier emphasis on grammar and translation, the approach was flawed in many ways, not the least of which was the problem that native speakers of the language had typically not memorized the same course book dialogue, and language learners had no other language to resort to when interlocutors did not stick to the dialogue! They did not learn how to negotiate meaning or ask for clarification. Ultimately, learners were not empowered to meet their own communicative goals through the audiolingual approach. Since that time, more comprehensive and effective approaches have risen to prominence, and we will discuss three here which suit the purposes of peacebuilding and reconciliation very well.

Communicative Language Teaching

Communicative language teaching (CLT) is simply the goal of enabling students to communicate meaningfully in their new language. While this may seem like an obvious goal for a language class, it was not always so. Language courses have often had grammar or word knowledge as the goal—which is a very different thing than being able to *use* the grammar and words for real communication. The approach of communicative language teaching is a very powerful one where peacebuilding and reconciliation are concerned. Instead of a lesson on future tense, for example, we might have a lesson on helping our neighbors. Students might be using sentences such as "I will walk my neighbor's dog" and "I will take my neighbor some bread." They are learning and using future tense, but the focus is on communication instead of grammar.

Task-based Language Teaching

When the goal is communication, it often works well to frame student communication activities as tasks. A communication task is something that the student tries to accomplish using language. For example, following the above lesson on *future tense*, the teacher might have a lesson on *past tense* with this as an end goal small group task: *Make a book showing and telling how you helped in your neighborhood.* Students would engage in helping their neighbors, take pictures, write text to accompany the pictures, and compile it all into a class book. Task-based language teaching can comprise a whole curriculum. One sample to look at is the *English for Life* curriculum (Dormer 2011; see resources in Appendix C). It is a five-level curriculum with tasks framed as "I can" statements, such as "I can write a letter telling about my family" or "I can tell a doctor my symptoms."

Task-based language teaching (TBLT) can provide many opportunities for incorporating peacebuilding goals. The above task about helping in one's neighborhood and then writing about it would have an added dimension of peacebuilding, for example, if students are engaging with neighbors who come from very different backgrounds than themselves, or perhaps about whom they may have held stereotypical views. Tasks can also be purposefully designed to engage in peacebuilding. Imagine, for example, a task to identify a communication problem in one's family and then lead in mediation efforts to work through the problem. As students prepare to engage in this task, they will be learning about both respectful communication and mediation, and then will have an opportunity to apply their learning to a real situation and report back to the class.

Content-based Language Teaching

When children around the world learn English by virtue of attending a school that is run in English, they are experiencing content-based language teaching (CBLT); that is, the learning of English by studying academic subjects in English. They are learning math, history, and science, but because all these subjects are taught in English, they also learn English. And content-based language learning is not limited to primary and secondary education—think about participating in a sports team, craft class, or Bible study where the common language is English. The fact is that learning English as a byproduct of studying something else in English has great potential, especially in terms of motivation.

Where peacebuilding and reconciliation are concerned, the opportunities afforded through content-based instruction are endless, as teachers can choose a content area that relates to such goals or that addresses issues such as conflict resolution, peer mediation, or peace concepts directly. For example, a middle school English class might instead be framed as a class on technology and friendship. Students might explore topics such as friending on Facebook, cyber-bullying, Snapchat, and other technology-mediated relationships. The teacher would embed appropriate tasks for acquiring and practicing English as students engage with the topics. In chapter 4, I (Jan) told about another content-based language teaching situation: a course on "the Christian family" given in Brazil. The adult learners in this course mostly attended the class in order to improve their English, but many expressed deep gratitude for learning about family relationships and communication.

An Eclectic Approach

These three approaches can all work together. For example, in the content-based technology and friendship course above, the goals are clearly communicative, and the teacher can organize the course content around tasks. These three in combination provide a powerful template for creating a course that will be effective for language acquisition, motivating for learners, and full of potential for reconciliation.

GROUPINGS

Intentional grouping of students to maximize language use and relationship-building is part and parcel of effective language teaching and the pursuit of peacebuilding. We will address three common student groupings here—whole class, small groups, and pairs—and provide sample activities and discussions of their application and use.

Whole Class Interaction

From the first ice-breaker to a final whole group discussion or presentation, there are times in most lessons for whole group interaction. Whole class interaction should not be confused with teacher-fronted classes in which the whole class is listening to the teacher. Such teacher-centered instruction should be minimized in language teaching and in teaching for the development of relationships. Whole class *interaction* involves activities in which students talk with one another, but they may also move around the classroom talking with different people or take turns contributing to an all-class discussion.

The types of whole class interaction which may be suitable depend very much on contextual factors such as the age and language level of the learners and the size of the class. In most classes, *ice-breakers* (for example, *find someone who . . .*) can be very effective in opening a class, providing an opportunity for light-hearted and congenial interactions to set the tone of the class. *Surveys* can also provide excellent opportunities for repeated but meaningful and authentic language use.

Whole class interaction can be an important first step in creating collaborative relationships in the classroom. Before students know each other well, these whole class activities provide students with greater latitude in choosing how much, when, and with whom they will speak or interact. Shyer students can hang back and watch until they feel more comfortable. Outgoing students can talk more and engage more people in conversation.

Group Work

One of the best connections between the teaching of English and teaching for reconciliation is that both are facilitated through work done in small groups—usually a grouping of three to five students. In language teaching, it is simply not possible to provide each student with the talk time needed in order to build speaking and conversation skill without utilizing small group and pair work. Likewise, as we seek opportunities for learners to build relationships and come to respect and understand each other better, individuals need time to dialogue on a more personal level than a whole class setting. There are many types of small group activities which work well for a variety of English levels and learning goals. Some of our favorites are *jigsaws, dicto-comp, group duties,* and *card sorts* (see Appendix A).

As you engage students in small group work, keep in mind the group dynamics already discussed in chapter 5. Here, we address group work from a more logistical and English language learning perspective, providing key concepts which may help to ensure that small group methodology not only meets English learning needs, but also achieves peacebuilding goals.

1. *Have a clearly defined task; explain and model it well.* In any English-learning setting students may have difficulty keeping conversation going. At lower language levels students may not have the English skills to just "discuss," without additional guidance. Further, if student groupings are made of individuals who may not automatically like each other, casual chatting may not be something students want to do. Outlining the task clearly, and providing it both orally and in writing, can ease the stress and make dialogue possible. For example, this prompt is vague: "Discuss the causes of pollution." This prompt is much more likely to lead to specific language use and discussion of the topic: "Write five statements beginning with *We can* telling some things you could do to reduce pollution."

2. *Give groups just enough time to complete the task.* Do not leave students in their groups after they have finished the task. That can lead to awkward silence or even frustration. Instead, let students know when they only have two to three minutes left to finish a task and conclude the task on time. In addition, always give groups that finish early something else to do, either additional group work, such as writing a summary or questions that emerged, or individual work, such as a homework assignment or reading. I (Jan) used to collect extra worksheets and cut up old English books for use in my "self-study box." When finished with a group task, students could go to this box and work on something that they felt would help them with their English.

3. *Change the profile of the groups.* Where English-learning goals are concerned, there are advantages to placing more advanced students with students at lower levels, but there are other advantages to placing students of similar abilities together. Where peacebuilding goals are concerned, there may be advantages to placing students together who struggle to get along, and there may be other advantages to placing best buddies together. Each type of grouping can have its advantages in accomplishing

the goals of a particular task, and it is critical when formulating student groups to understand and consider all the elements of identity and group dynamics that were discussed in chapter 5. It is also important to have a clear idea of what you hope the task will accomplish. Are students creating a dialogue for a role-play? Perhaps you will want mixed ability groups, where a student who is more advanced can have more speaking parts than a lower level student. Are students sharing about a difficult time in their lives? Perhaps you will want to put good friends and similar English levels together to facilitate discussion that may be a little difficult. Intentionality in grouping is the key.

Pair Work

Pair work can be easier to navigate logistically, as it may be easier for two people to find a place to sit and work together. An *interview* is an example of a pair activity which can be utilized across language and age levels and for many different learning objectives. Consider the ideas below in utilizing pair work:

1. *Use pair work to elicit non-threatening speaking.* One of the greatest advantages of pair work in language acquisition is that it compels students to speak. When there are only two in a conversation, even reluctant speakers will usually try to engage rather than endure awkward silence. At the same time, speaking to an audience of one other person significantly lowers the stress factor involved in speaking in a new language.
2. *Ensure good understanding of the task.* Just as clarity is important in group tasks, it is even more important in pair work, as there are fewer people to work together to understand what is to be done. It is awkward to sit beside another person silently, not knowing what to do.
3. *Use intentional pairings.* Intentionality in creating small groups was discussed above. When placing students in pairs, the same issues apply. However, in pairing students, even more attention should be given to the emotional factors which may be present. When two people have no choice but to speak to each other

and work together, the teacher should consider carefully how to pair students who *can* and *will* engage in the desired work together. Teachers sometimes revert to having students "talk to the person next to you." If seating has not been intentional, this may not be the most effective way to pair students.

4. *"Self, pair, group" is a good sequence.* For many tasks, it works well to begin by letting students think on their own, then have them share in pairs, and then share with a larger group. For example, suppose I want students to practice statements with *should* while at the same time thinking about ways to build classroom community. I might assign the task, "Write three rules you think we should have in this class. Begin each rule with *everyone should* or *no one should.*" Instead of moving directly to a small group task, I might first ask students to write their own three rules. Then I would have them share those rules with one other person and, as they do so, possibly modify their rule or language. Finally, two pairs would come together forming a group, and all four would finalize the three rules that their group would present.

ACTIVITIES

After selecting the overall approach for a course or class, the teacher will be planning units, then individual lessons. Keeping in mind the tips concerning student groupings above, the teacher will select activities that students will engage in to use the English language and pursue the possible peacebuilding goals that have been integrated into the lesson. In chapter 6 we learned the acronym "REAL" as an evaluative lens for methodology. To re-cap, REAL activities are:

FIG. 3: REAL ACTIVITIES IN TEACHING ENGLISH FOR RECONCILIATION

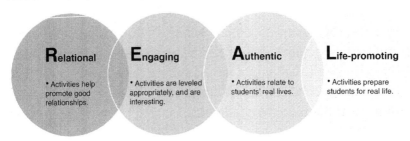

Relational
* Activities help promote good relationships.

Engaging
* Activities are leveled appropriately, and are interesting.

Authentic
* Activities relate to students' real lives.

Life-promoting
* Activities prepare students for real life.

Activities in Appendix A

In Appendix A, many activities fitting the REAL criteria are described. We selected activities for inclusion in this book that are relatively simple to understand, that can be used across a wide range of age groups and language proficiency levels, and that require little preparation and few materials. We suggest that teachers actively try out each of these in the classroom to become familiar with them. As you learn which ones "fit" your teaching style and context, you may focus in on eight to twelve "go to" activities that you are able to develop quickly and use with ease. Having such a "go to" list can raise a teacher's comfort level in teaching, lessen the load of preparation, and ultimately increase satisfaction and longevity in the classroom.

Songs and Chants

A final type of activity which bears special mention because of its strong potential in reconciliatory classrooms is the use of songs and chants. We have rarely seen an English language classroom in which the use of songs and chants was not effective. Songs are especially helpful as we pursue relational goals in the classroom. People all over the world appreciate music; there is something about it that speaks to us on an emotional level. It is this deeper ability of music to speak to the soul that makes it a great resource for language classes which have reconciliatory goals. Here are some examples of how songs can be used in an English learning classroom:

1. Students are provided with a melody and are given the task to work in groups to write lyrics on the topic of peace.
2. Students are given a task to listen to different kinds of music and then write how the music makes them feel.
3. Students learn new vocabulary and structures because they learn them in a song and sing the song frequently enough in class to commit it to memory.
4. Students listen to the song "Lean on Me" (see Appendix A), filling in the missing lyrics as they listen. They then complete

the remainder of the worksheet, which helps them learn idioms, and ultimately leads them to consider how they "lean on" others and how others can "lean on" them.

5. Chants are basically songs without music. They are fun, catchy, and can provide much-needed repetition so that English learners develop automaticity in using new language. But chants can also be a way to help learners gain comfort and automaticity in using key phrases that can facilitate positive relationships. The "Forgiveness Chant" in Chapter 6 is one such example.

SUMMARY OF METHODOLOGIES

The approaches, groupings, and activities discussed in this section have hopefully provided a starting point for envisioning how methodology is instrumental in making possible the reconciliatory goals in an English-learning classroom. Appendix A provides many useful activities, and Appendix B provides a sample unit and lesson plan showing how methodologies can be utilized in instructional planning. We also welcome dialogue with readers and are happy to point you in the direction of further resources! (See author contact information in the back of the book.)

SKILLS: MODEL AND TEACH SKILLS TO ENHANCE CONFLICT RESOLUTION AND INTERCULTURAL COMMUNICATION.

One of the most significant connections between language teaching and teaching for peace and reconciliation is that in both the ultimate goal is *skill,* not merely *knowledge.* As discussed in chapter 2, teaching for language acquisition is unlike teaching academic content. In language teaching, acquiring information—the words and structures in the language—is not the end goal, but rather *using* those words and structures for real communication. This use of language constitutes the development of skills: reading, writing, speaking, and listening.

Similarly, there are specific skills used for engaging in reconciliation that include the ability to engage in respectful dialogue, knowing how to use words and phrases that show value for the other person, and even skills in rephrasing and requesting clarification in order to increase understanding. Some reconciliatory skills involve language directly, while others may relate to language, but actually point to broader skills that can transfer from students' and teachers' past experiences. Table 1 shows some different types of reconciliatory skills with examples of the kinds of language and other skills required. When designing a unit or lesson plan with reconciliatory goals in mind, it can be helpful to identify which language skills could be a focus for a lesson and which other skills could be practiced at the same time, recognizing that the other skills may or may not already be part of the students' repertoires.

TABLE: ALIGNING SKILL SETS FOR RECONCILIATORY GOALS

Type of reconciliatory skills	English language skills required	Other skills required
Conflict resolution	Expressing opinions sensitively, restating and paraphrasing, checking understanding, restating meaning, listening actively	Clarifying issues, remaining calm in conflict situations, showing respect for differences, collaborating, compromising
Mediation and negotiation	Describing a situation in detail, agreeing and disagreeing, summarizing, listening for common ground, taking notes from dialogue	Focusing on deeper needs and interests instead of positions, envisioning alternative options, brainstorming, finding sources of power
Trauma sensitivity	Talking about difficult topics, listening actively and deeply, speaking without judgment, clarifying understanding, describing behavior	Caring for self and others' well-being, showing flexibility, focusing on strengths instead of weaknesses
Restorative justice	Facilitating dialogue, speaking with respect, showing concern for others, asking questions, writing a contract	Focusing on harms done, demonstrating support, empowering others, problem-solving, forgiving

Type of reconciliatory skills	English language skills required	Other skills required
Nonviolent communication	Speaking about feelings, listening carefully, identifying underlying needs, using nonviolent vocabulary, speaking without judgment	Recognizing feelings, identifying nonverbal communication, demonstrating empathy and compassion
Organizational leadership	Leading a team, taking turns, keeping on task, dealing with interruptions, opening and closing group dialogue	Analyzing conflict, strategic planning, addressing conflict directly, using appropriate settings for communication
Intercultural communication	Initiating conversation, adapting speech to listener, clarifying meaning, explaining aspects of culture, apologizing	Tolerating cultural discomfort, developing awareness of own identities and cultures, challenging stereotypes
Coaching and facilitation	Listening carefully, asking open-ended questions, reflecting questions, inviting others to speak, balancing talk time	Using creativity, demonstrating flexibility, monitoring group dynamics, refraining from giving answers, setting goals
Relationship and community building	Sharing stories connected to others, inviting others to events, engaging in meaningful small talk, working together on a project	Noticing opportunities for connections, creating opportunities for fun together, including others
Social and emotional literacy	Communicating feelings, using silence appropriately, talking about self and others, collaborative decision-making	Monitoring nonverbal communication of self and others, using humor appropriately, regulating own emotions, developing self-awareness

Just as language *learning* is skill-based, good language *teaching* is in large part a skill set as well. Planning well prior to class is only half of the challenge in language teaching. The other half is the real-time interaction and the minute-by-minute decision-making that a teacher engages in, to increase learning potential for his or her students. Where teaching English for reconciliation is concerned, teachers need two sets of skills: the ability to foster language acquisition and the ability to model and teach the reconciliatory skills mentioned above.

So, skills are constantly being used, modeled, practiced, and learned in the English language classroom where reconciliation is also a goal. The teacher uses good English teaching skills and may be learning and growing in the understanding and modeling of reconciliatory skills, integrated into the very fabric of the English class. The students are learning language skills, even as they are seeing reconciliatory skills modeled by the teacher, and are given opportunities to develop these skills themselves. There are many different types of skills that may be modeled, taught, and practiced in an English for reconciliation classroom. Here, we address just a few of them in two categories: the skill set of the teacher, and the skills that teachers may want to actively try to help learners develop.

SKILLS OF THE TEACHER

One of the most important skill sets for an English teacher to develop is that of providing feedback in response to students' efforts to use the language. Corrective feedback is important in language learning, but knowing if, how, and when to provide it is a complex skill set. What counts as an "error," and when and how students are ready to correct it, depends very much on the context, as well as what variety of English students need to know and use in order to pursue their goals. Keeping all this in mind, there will be times when corrective feedback is needed, as students who do not receive enough feedback to help them continue to grow in their use of the language are at risk of developing *fossilized* errors. This need for feedback in order to grow in language provides the reconciliatory English teacher with many opportunities to interact with learners while modeling helpful, affirming, and empowering interactions. For example, let's imagine that a student is struggling to pronounce the word "van," and instead is saying "ban." We can probably all envision a stereotypical language teacher getting close to the learner's face, repeating "van," "VAN," **"VAN,"** louder and louder. We may even have been on the receiving end of such teacher efforts when trying to learn a new language! But this kind of feedback is not modeling respectful, empowering interaction. A better way forward might be to provide the learner with tools that he can use to understand the pronunciation of "v" and to check his own pronunciation. The teacher who knows how to provide this kind of feedback might take out a hand mirror, show the student how to look for the placement of the upper teeth on the bottom lip to correctly make the "v" sound, then provide the learner with some time to practice on his own with the mirror.

Another skill set that English teachers need is that of adapting to and accommodating the voices, needs, and ideas that emerge during the course of a language lesson. I (Jan) have always felt that some of my best teaching was unplanned! It often came about because of a question or a need voiced by a student. A good language teacher is able to balance the need to teach the stated lesson with the need to adapt the lesson to emerging realities. This provides another excellent convergence with reconciliatory goals, as these, too, require sensitivity to the feelings and needs of the people in the room. For example, in one class of adult learners in Indonesia, a mother had brought her two-month-old baby to class. The baby was fussy, and the mother was distraught. I could have asked that she take the baby out into the hallway, as the class was being disrupted. Instead, I had the class of eight students, several mothers themselves, gather around her. They were able to practice English by providing advice (lots of it!), and I could see that the mother of the baby was beginning to relax, feeling surrounded and supported by friends. At the end, I asked her if I could pray for her baby. She was extremely grateful for the prayer, and it proved to be a turning point in her life. She went on to become a strong Christian and an English teacher with goals of reconciliation in difficult contexts.

A final teaching skill that we will address here is that of designing the physical space for both language acquisition and reconciliation.

We have taught in many places where the physical space is seemingly unchangeable. In some classrooms, the desks or tables take up most of the available classroom space and may even be bolted to the floor. Sometimes the movement of chairs on the floor is very noisy (not to mention the movement of children!) and creating such noise in schools where all the doors and windows are open and noise carries easily is frowned upon or even banned. Still, in most classrooms, we have found that there are ways to orchestrate the movement of students for the different groupings mentioned above. There are ways to ensure that students have opportunities to look at and interact with one another, rather than sitting in rows, facing the front of the classroom. This traditional type of classroom arrangement does not promote the relationship-building that those who teach English for reconciliation will want to see happen during at least some parts of the class. Elementary school classrooms in Indonesia are typically of the variety where most classroom space is filled with desks, and all students face the front. Yet even in those kinds of classrooms, I (Jan) have rarely found a classroom in which I could not have students gather in small circles along the sides of the classroom, or in the hallways, for more relational activities such as *circle practice* (see appendix A). Often, there *is* a way to make the classroom space more conducive to interaction.

SKILLS OF THE LEARNERS

English learners' main task in acquiring the English language is usually that of developing the skills of reading, writing, speaking, and listening in English. These are interactive, relational skills. When students read, they are interacting with the writer and with the content. When students write, they are writing for a particular audience. When students speak and listen, the interaction through oral communication is obvious. It is this nature of language as interactive and relational that integrates so well with reconciliatory goals, as these are also about relating to and interacting with others. Here, we want to address some more specific learner skills which achieve the goals of both language learning and peacebuilding. Although there are many peacebuilding skills that could be part of an English class, we will focus on conflict resolution skills and intercultural communication as they can overlap with many of the other types of reconciliatory skills listed in Table 1.

Conflict resolution skills involve the ability to recognize, navigate, and effectively address a conflict situation. This may or may not result in actually resolving the conflict; at a minimum, conflicts can be managed to avoid causing more harm, or at best they can be transformed into opportunities for growth and learning for all. The language skills that enable this to happen often appear as part of English teaching curriculum and materials. When students learn to express their opinions sensitively, restate what they hear from others to check their own understanding, ask open-ended questions, or summarize information from discussion, they are also learning skills that will help in situations of conflict. Teachers can design tasks such as role-plays, which set up opportunities for students to practice these skills, as well as practice other aspects of dealing with conflict such as reflecting others' feelings and validating others' concerns.

Another set of skills that are important for language learners are intercultural communication skills. By nature, English language learning requires interacting with people from different cultures. Students can practice initiating conversation with people they do not know and explaining aspects of their own cultures. Depending on your context, this can be a fun topic to use with the *Concentric Circles* activity. Other aspects of intercultural communication include adapting one's speaking to the listener, which could lead to exploration of different pronunciations, what makes pronunciation clear in your setting, and strategies to clarify meaning when the person you are talking with cannot understand what you are saying. During activities that practice these skills, students also have a chance to build awareness of their own identities and cultures and challenge stereotypes that arise. Teachers can model intercultural communication by not avoiding discussion of cultural differences or stereotypes, but instead exploring them further by prompting more explanation of what experiences might have led to those stereotypes and creating space for others in the class to share stories of alternate experiences.

ISSUES: FRAME THEMES, TOPICS, AND MATERIALS WITH A PEACE PERSPECTIVE

In many English teaching contexts, the teacher has the freedom to choose at least some of the themes, topics, and materials used in the class. In some settings, teachers have total freedom to gear English classes to meet the needs and interests of the students through purposeful selection of the teaching topics and resources. In others, there may be a grammar-based curriculum specifying learning goals such as "prepositions" or "past tense," but the teacher may have freedom to choose the topics of discussion or readings to practice using prepositions or past tense. In yet other settings, topics may be prescribed, such as "health" or "family," and as teachers prepare individual lessons, they may have latitude to further refine such topics as "healthy responses to stress" or "helping in the family," and to choose their own materials to elaborate on these themes. Of course, in some contexts, course books are prescribed, and there is little choice over themes, topics, or materials. In chapter 8 we look at recourses for the reconciliatory teacher in those situations. In this chapter, we are thinking of contexts in which the teacher has some choice and can frame themes, topics, and materials with a peace perspective.

THEMES AND TOPICS

The ability to select the topics used in English classes is one of the main reasons for the good fit between teaching English and teaching for reconciliation. This is not possible in most other types of classrooms. If one is teaching history or science, for example, the content of that class is fairly prescribed. Not so in teaching language. Students simply need to use the new language, and generally are open to a wide range of topics as they learn to use it. So, how does the reconciliatory English teacher go about making the most of this opportunity? Following are some ideas to consider:

1. Take inventory of students' interests and felt needs. Adult learners may need to acquire certain vocabulary sets or functional language abilities for their professions or for integrating into new communities. Younger learners may have specific interests such as soccer or a popular band. All groups of learners may have varied preferences due to personalities or hobbies. Knowing your learners well is the first step in choosing themes and topics that will appeal to them and motivate them.

2. Consider the selected themes or topics through a reconciliatory lens. If soccer is of interest to learners, for example, is there a related ethical or relational issue that could provide good opportunities for discussion and reflection? One textbook for children in an EFL context (Dormer 2012) has a story about Carlos, who is playing soccer with his friends when the ball touches his hand. However, no one sees this, and so the game continues. But Carlos is bothered by his lack of honesty. The textbook has students suggest what Carlos should do. Students learn to make suggestions using the words *should, could,* and *might,* but at the same time they are processing an ethical dilemma and may identify with Carlos's inner struggles over his identity and the kind of person he wants to be.

3. Consider overt topics related to peacebuilding, even if students have not suggested these themes. Many students have never thought or heard much about skills in conflict resolution or peacebuilding and would likely not think of these as possible topics for an English class. This does not mean, however, that they would not be open to and learn from such topics. In an intermediate-level class of young adults preparing for further studies or professional careers, for example, acquiring the skills to resolve conflicts and build good relationships with others, alongside their learning of English, can only be helpful.

MATERIALS

As discussed in chapter 6, those new to English teaching sometimes erroneously believe that getting the right materials is their main task. Though we saw that the characteristics of the teacher are actually much more important than the materials chosen, eventually there does come a time to consider what materials, if any, to use. Materials selected must further the curricular goals and meet the real needs of the learners. A good way to think about materials is to consider how they are best used in one of these ways:

- As homework, to further learning outside of class (e.g. a text to read at home)
- As a resource to facilitate interaction in class (such as some of the sample materials in Appendix A)
- As a learning tool for using new words and structures and a resource to refer back to when engaged in individual study.

So, if there is a curriculum or unit plan (see Appendix B) in place and the teacher has adopted appropriate methodologies, themes, and topics, the last piece of the puzzle in teaching English for reconciliation may be finding or designing appropriate learner materials. In chapter 8 we address contexts in which course materials are already provided and possibly even mandated. In this chapter, we are talking about situations in which the teacher has freedom to create or find materials that will meet the needs of the learners. Many English learning materials are available online and in published form as well. The teacher seeking to integrate peacebuilding goals into English classes may also want to investigate peacebuilding and conflict resolution materials and adapt them for English language learners (see sources in Appendix C). Following are some tips to remember when selecting, modifying, or designing materials.

TIPS FOR FURTHERING ENGLISH LEARNING AND PEACEBUILDING GOALS THROUGH MATERIALS DEVELOPMENT:

1. Make sure worksheets "function" well. Limit the density of text on a page for English language learners, particularly when adapting peace education materials written for fully proficient English users. Make sure that blanks are the right size

for responses, there is enough space between lines for hand-writing, and fonts are easy to read.

2. Keep in mind the language level of the learners. Especially remember to keep any instructions clear and direct. For example, instead of "Identify the synonyms for conflict in the sentences below" simply write "Underline the words that mean *conflict.*" If instructions on peace education materials are too complex, re-create the handout or write simpler instructions on the board instead.

3. Utilize pictures, illustrations, graphs, charts, and tables. All of these can aid in comprehension and lessen the stress of facing a daunting page of text in a foreign language. However, be sure to view all pictures and graphics through a lens of cultural sensitivity and contextual awareness. For example, in a unit on cooking, a large Western kitchen with modern appliances may not be an appropriate photo. A more modest representation of a basic, functional kitchen may better represent the learners' (and possibly the teacher's) reality.

4. Use humor! Cartoons, funny pictures, and playful icons can all help to lighten the mood of a language class and increase enjoyment. However, again, make these selections considering the cultures of the students. Humor that pokes fun at anyone or any culture, whether represented in the group or not, is not helpful and can be very counter-productive.

5. Use multimedia. If internet and computer access is available, using videos, images, and interactive sites online can provide different ways to engage a topic and present multiple perspectives. Even if computer technology is not available, using multiple forms of materials, such as real items, audio, and three-dimensional models can spark creativity and new ways of interacting.

6. Involve the students. Get learners to do as much of the work as possible as part of the lesson tasks. Learners can research topics online to find articles or images; put together graphic organizers of information; or design their own dialogues, role-plays, games, or worksheets for each other. Developing their

own materials, or portions thereof, provides more opportunities for language learning and empowerment and can provide a natural opportunity for collaboration. It also nurtures student creativity, an essential part of peacebuilding, and can provide space for ways of thinking that might be on the margins.

RELATIONSHIPS: CONTINUALLY MONITOR AND PRIORITIZE RELATIONSHIPS

The central element in our framework is relationships: the heart of teaching English for reconciliation. In this area, too, language teaching shares a fundamental value with reconciliatory skills and actions. In both, people must be connected and engaged with each other. In English learning classrooms, if the people in the room are not talking with one another, then communicative skills are not being developed. And if people are not in dialogue, peacebuilding is likely not occurring either. So, what can the reconciliatory English teacher do to continually monitor and prioritize relationships? We will look at two ways forward here.

CONSTANT ATTENTIVENESS TO CLASSROOM RELATIONSHIPS

With a focus on reconciliation comes a shift from focusing primarily on the academic part of class to a focus on the individuals in the class, their relationships with one another, and their feelings about their relationships with one another. A teacher who is attentive to relationships will, for example, monitor group work differently than a teacher focused purely on language learning. The reconciliatory teacher will listen not only to the language being used, but also to hesitations, silences, and interruptions, constantly interpreting the relating that is occurring. This teacher will watch for nonverbal signals, recognizing the cultures of the students so as to not misinterpret these nonverbal signals. This relationship-fostering teacher will care deeply how students are feeling in class, will never feel that it is okay to have students who are marginalized or silenced in class, and will constantly work towards providing opportunities for all voices to be heard, valued, and supported.

PRIORITIZING RELATIONSHIPS IN DECISION-MAKING IN ALL AREAS ABOVE

Throughout this chapter we have seen many of the areas in which teachers make decisions, whether at the planning stage or when making real-time decisions in the classroom. The reconciliatory teacher keeps "relationships" front and center as a main lens through which all choices are viewed. This teacher chooses class-room approaches, methodologies, themes, and materials while thinking constantly about which will promote strong relation-ships inside and outside of class. Sometimes, the prioritization of relationships may mean veering from the planned lesson, and allowing other, unplanned discourse to take place in the class. Sometimes it may even mean opening up to students more than teachers normally do, modeling authenticity and vulnerability.

I (Jan) experienced just such a class one time in Kenya. I taught English for theology in a seminary, and my students were young to middle-aged adults in or preparing for ministry. After a year there, my husband and I endured a devastating experience in ministry. I went to class that day, determined to teach as usual and to achieve the learning objectives on my lesson plan. Somehow, I thought it would not be right to share with my students on such a personal level. But the students knew something was wrong, and just a few minutes into the class, one wise student ventured, "Mwalimu, tell us what is wrong." I did, and that day, my students shared my hurt, and my burden was lightened. I was not able to tell them all the details of what had happened, but I was able to be real with them, and they ministered to me. My relationship with several students in that class was deepened so much through that time of sharing that they remain in contact with me to this day.

A focus on relationships can never go wrong. It can be hard, but the focus on relationships will only make English language acquisi-tion more effective, and it has the potential for furthering reconcil-iatory goals as well.

PRACTICAL APPLICATION: TOOLS FOR TEACHING ENGLISH FOR RECONCILIATORY PURPOSES

1. *Understand the broader systems and context before planning instruction.* Who are the learners? What systems have they come from and what systems surround them now? What is their language level? What transitional and emotional issues are they facing? What factors related to peacebuilding might arise in the English class? The context-planning form provided in Appendix B may be helpful in understanding the broader systems and context.
2. *Select methodologies which facilitate language learning and reconciliation goals.* In this chapter, we have suggested approaches and groupings which work well for both language development and teaching for reconciliation. We have suggested the REAL acronym as a way to select appropriate activities. Many activities that we have found to be helpful in teaching English for reconciliation can be found in Appendix A.
3. *Utilize effective English-teaching skills and model peacebuilding skills.* Empower learners by providing learner-focused feedback. Develop the skills of appropriate flexibility, accommodation, and classroom management. Model conflict resolution and intercultural communication, and create opportunities for students to practice these skills as well.
4. *Select topics, themes, and materials which further both the English learning and reconciliatory goals that you have targeted.* Utilize the lists provided in this chapter for identifying appropriate topics and creating, adapting, or finding useful materials.
5. *Prioritize relationships!* Realize that the most important thing in any classroom is the people in it. Create classroom environments, procedures, and plans in which students have opportunities to build relationships.

CONCLUSION

If you are new to English language teaching, we hope that this look at teaching English through our reconciliatory framework has been helpful. While the main focus of this book is not learning how to teach English, it hopefully nevertheless points you in the direction of some good methodologies that you can start with. You may want to take some time at this point to look through the resources provided in all of the appendices and to connect those resources with your learning through this chapter. For both novice and veteran English language teachers, we hope that this chapter has fleshed out what teaching English for reconciliation may look like. If the many ideas presented here and in the appendices seem overwhelming, we suggest that you focus on just one or two areas to apply to your teaching. For example, you may decide to give more considered thought to learner pairs and engage in very purposeful pairing over your next few lessons. When that type of planning becomes second nature, another issue can be addressed. If you implement these suggestions bit by bit, over time you will find that your classroom has become very conducive to both English language acquisition and peacebuilding.

CHAPTER 8

ADAPTING CURRICULA FOR PEACE AND RECONCILIATION

INTRODUCTION

Several years ago, I (Cheryl) was asked to teach a group of adults who were required to take a test of spoken English as a part of the process to become flight attendants for a prestigious airline. All of them had already passed the first stages of the application process and the demanding English test was the next challenge to overcome. The students were focused on their goals, the curriculum and textbook were set, and I was to teach. As an educator invested in teaching English for reconciliation, how could I possibly integrate my ideals for peacebuilding into this class? Besides the fact that the curriculum was already established and the students were not interested in peacebuilding, we were already short on time before we started! At the time, I didn't have any clear ideas about how to integrate or infuse peacebuilding into the course, so I just kept my focus on helping the students achieve their goals while also reflecting consistently on what peace education could look like in each lesson. Interestingly, by the end of the class, not only did all of the students reach their goal of passing the test, but we had also created a community of relationships that actually rose above the intense competition in the world of flight attendant applicants. Students who had taken the class and who ended up competing against one another maintained their friendship through it all. Several even took another content-based course about peacebuilding!

What happened in this class that led to such positive relationship building? The previous chapter looked at strategies, techniques, and ideas for teaching a class for reconciliation where teachers have flexibility in curriculum. This chapter looks at situations like the one above in which the curriculum is assigned or perhaps where students' primary goals may not necessarily include learning about peace and reconciliation.

INITIAL CONSIDERATIONS

Before getting into the specifics of adapting curriculum to teach for reconciliation, a few points are important to emphasize. First, recognizing and responding to students' needs, both as the teacher perceives these needs and as students themselves understand these needs, is a critical part of teaching with integrity. Teaching for reconciliation does not happen when teachers ignore what students see as their need in order to address only the needs the teacher perceives. That is, if students are in the class to address their need for academic reading, it does not aid reconciliation for the teacher to insist their need is actually reconciliation. In fact, this mismatch at best leads to misunderstandings and at worst can actually destroy relationships and move further from peace and reconciliation in the classroom! Recognizing student needs as they perceive them, and doing our best as teachers to help them meet their needs, is the first step in reconciliation of teachers and students in an academic culture often filled with conflict and power imbalances.

Second, a related point is that teachers working for reconciliation cannot have secret agendas for peace education hidden from students. While it may not be appropriate to highlight every task's relevance to peacebuilding, teachers should be transparent about their interest in peace and reconciliation and how that influences the class.[4] This may mean deeper discussions as a class about how students might see reconciliation as relevant to their learning or

---

[4] For more on the importance of transparency in any kind of English teaching ministry, see Dormer 2011.

simply pointing out how healthy relationships assist in language learning. Of course, explanations of this aspect of the curriculum must be appropriate to age and language proficiency. In any case, it is important to be as open as possible concerning your goals and objectives for the class and why you have these goals and objectives.

Finally, peace education is ideally built on collaboration and a spirit of reconciliation among teaching colleagues and administration. While teachers do not need to announce a "peace agenda" to the whole school, talking about peace issues in class or teaching conflict resolution skills will not be very effective if peacebuilding is not modeled in our professional relationships. This means that we should not avoid conflict by ignoring negative feedback or giving up on our efforts if challenged, but rather use the skills and tools we are trying to teach, rooted in values of respect and authentic listening, to engage others in ways that seek to transform conflict. We should be willing to practice self-reflection and model the principle of "peace starts with me." This can sometimes be a challenge if a teacher does not get support from other teachers or administration, even to the point of push back from colleagues or resistance to change. While it might not be easy to deal with push back or challenges from colleagues, bearing in mind that peace is not only the destination, but also the path, helps to keep the whole effort in perspective. To build peace, we need to do the hard work of engaging conflict in healthy ways rather than avoiding it or letting it escalate until harm is done. The path to reconciliation is the way of peace and our interactions with our colleagues have ripple effects that reach the students and beyond.

WORKING WITH EXISTING CURRICULUM

Given these caveats, there are still many contexts in which teachers may find it appropriate to adapt existing curriculum to a reconciliatory perspective. You may not have either the time to design your own peace education course or the flexibility to use existing peace education curriculum. Perhaps you have been directed to teach a specific curriculum with clear course goals, unit or lesson plans, assignments, materials, and assessments. Whatever the situation, you can still plan and teach English for reconciliation in your context. The framework in Figure 4 can help teachers seeking to infuse their existing curriculum with opportunities for reconciliation and peace education. The following paragraphs describe each element of the framework in more detail, propose some questions to frame an inquiry of the curriculum, and provide examples of each element in practice.

Fig. 4: Reconciliatory English Teaching Framework

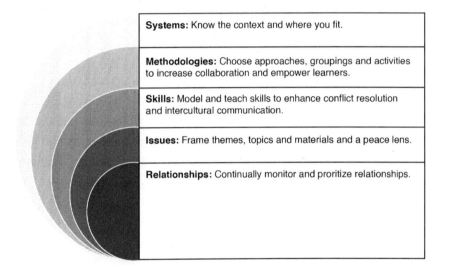

Systems: Know the context and where you fit.

Methodologies: Choose approaches, groupings and activities to increase collaboration and empower learners.

Skills: Model and teach skills to enhance conflict resolution and intercultural communication.

Issues: Frame themes, topics and materials and a peace lens.

Relationships: Continually monitor and proritize relationships.

Systems: Know the Context and Where You Fit

Before adapting curricula to integrate peace perspectives, it is essential to complete the contextual analysis as described in chapter 7. Only after knowing the context, learner identities, and learner needs can teachers begin to adapt a curriculum to meet those needs. In addition, when coming into a program in which the curriculum is already set, it is important to ask why your course is designed the way it is. Considering the goals that the curriculum writers had in mind can help us recognize where we fit in the context and how our position might influence our students. Questions to ask about the course design and curriculum include:

- What is it about the context that has led administration to put together this course and select this curriculum? How could those reasons influence how well students learn?
- How am I positioned as teacher in this curriculum? Does this position support or restrict me in empowering learners and creating space for reconciliation?
- How well do the larger purposes of this course and curriculum align with peacebuilding and reconciliatory goals in the context? Will my teaching contribute to the ministry of reconciliation on a larger scale as well?

Answering these questions draws attention to larger goals or outcomes of the curriculum, which may be either openly acknowledged or unspoken. They can also help us to realistically envision our part as a teacher in the program and reflect on how that might influence our teaching.

I (Jan) once taught an advanced level speaking class in a university's intensive English program in the United States. The textbooks and curriculum were prescribed and included a text on formal speaking, which was not written for English learners, and another text on idioms. I surmised that the administration had chosen these texts because students needed to develop skills in giving oral presentations in an academic setting and students felt they needed to better understand idioms. My position as a teacher was primarily to ensure that students learned how to give academic presentations. I felt that this goal afforded me space to pursue reconciliatory goals, as I had latitude in working with students on the *topics* of those presentations. I was able to design the topic selection part of the process in such a way as to foster deep reflection on students' identities and their difficulties in acculturating to life in an American university. The majority of the students in the class were secular Chinese and two were from Saudi Arabia and were Muslim. One of these Muslim students shared with me in a one-on-one session how misunderstood he felt among the other students and Americans who were not Muslim. I urged him to create his oral presentation on the topic of Islam, with his purpose being to help others understand Islam. He did pursue this topic, gave a stellar informative presentation, and at the end many of the Chinese students pursued further understanding by asking authentic questions. Because of the Muslim student's presentation, one of the Chinese students gained the confidence to announce that he was a Christian and gave his own presentation on the house church movement in China. Much to my relief, the other Chinese students in the class were genuinely interested. I felt that, in this class, larger goals of reconciliation and understanding *were* achieved, despite the restrictions of a set curriculum.

METHODOLOGIES: CHOOSE APPROACHES, GROUPINGS, AND ACTIVITIES TO INCREASE COLLABORATION AND EMPOWER LEARNERS

Methods are often not specified directly in a curriculum, so teachers may have some flexibility in selecting methodologies. As described in chapter 7, ways of teaching that promote collaboration rather than competition and that give learners the greatest possible chance to make their own decisions and take ownership of their learning, will more likely create opportunities for peacebuilding and reconciliation. Questions to help in adapting the approaches and methods of a curriculum include:

- What approaches are specified or suggested by the curriculum materials and resources? Are they communicative, content-based, or task-based? If not, can they be shaped to be more aligned with these approaches, such as reworking an assignment to require authentic communication or eliciting content from students around which to frame the course?
- How well do the methods and activities create opportunities for building relationships among students? How can I shift the methods to include more collaboration instead of competition or isolated activities?
- How do the methods and activities invite student participation and empower them in the class and beyond? How

can I change task instructions to increase student decision making appropriate to the context?

Answers to these questions can help teachers to gauge which methods may need refining to add elements of collaboration or reduce competition, to move a step back to include learners in decision making related to the class activities, and to think about ways in which empowerment can move beyond the classroom.

For instance, program administrators at an English peace camp for children and youth that I (Cheryl) worked with had developed a curriculum they were using to train teachers and create materials. They asked me to help look at the suggested activities and revise the curriculum according to best language-teaching methods and peace education methods. This particular curriculum included a lot of instruction for teachers, as they were often inexperienced volunteers. However, the methods the curriculum used were mainly teacher-centered, focused on the teacher at the front of the room. There were a number of lectures, stories, and role-plays, but all delivered by the teachers. A few games were woven in, but they were often competitive. One even had the winners punishing the losers at the end! There was little group work and students had few opportunities to make any choices, other than during individual art project tasks.

After meeting together with the program administrators and a few of the lead teachers, we worked through the whole curriculum, adding more group work options, adapting the competitive games to collaborative ones, and designing tasks so that students could be at the center of the communication and make decisions about their learning. The result was much more English language being used and learned by the campers, less stress on the volunteer teachers, and much more fun and collaboration during the lessons at camp.

Even when the curriculum is fairly rigid, tweaking aspects of the methods, activities, and tasks according to peacebuilding approaches can do much to shift the whole dynamic of the class.

Skills: Model and Teach Skills to Enhance Conflict Resolution and Intercultural Communication

In any language learning curriculum, language skills are part of the focus. However, teachers can choose how to frame those skills and whether to add an emphasis on those that align with conflict resolution skills and intercultural communication that build understanding. Some questions to consider in relation to skills include:

- Which skills from the curriculum overlap with skills for conflict resolution and intercultural communication? Do lesson objectives include skills that can reinforce or be a starting point for peacebuilding skills, such as negotiating meaning, checking understanding, apologizing, expressing feelings and explanations, listening actively, finding points of view in reading, and writing for a diverse audience?
- How can additional skills for conflict resolution and intercultural communication be integrated alongside the skills that are already being practiced (see Table 1 in chapter 7)?
- Are there skills currently being practiced that contrast with skills for conflict resolution and intercultural communication and might require some reflection? Can I model intercultural communication and conflict resolution skills in leading this reflection? For example, can I facilitate critical reflection on the difference between debate and dialogue skills in escalating conflict? Can we explore different cultural perspectives about critical thinking? Can I teach grammar skills as conventions for specific contexts, instead of a set of rules to follow, in order to value different cultural ways of speaking and writing English?

Answers to these questions can help teachers focus on modeling and teaching skills that promote peacebuilding and can prompt reflection on skills being taught that may limit conflict resolution and intercultural communication.

An example of this focus on skills occurred within the context of a high intermediate grammar class that I (Cheryl) taught at an intensive English program at a university in the United States. The curriculum guide and textbook that we were assigned had short units focused on different grammar points with a few communicative tasks at the end of each lesson. Although the framing of the chapter was on the grammar point, in practice many of the skills in the book overlapped with skills for conflict resolution or intercultural communication. For instance, the unit on tag questions, such as "don't you?" and "isn't it?" fit well with checking understanding and sorting out misunderstandings. Instead of starting with presenting the grammar point, we began with the communicative exercise and elicited methods for checking understanding, including strategies other than tag questions. In our practice of tag questions, one student asked about the expression "don't it," which he had heard from a local friend. This prompted some reflection on non-standard Englishes, and other students shared whether tag questions existed in the same way in other languages they knew. I facilitated this conversation with the use of open-ended questions and careful paraphrasing of student responses, trying to nurture our interest in different cultural groups and language variations. Rather than emphasizing what is right or wrong, we ended the class recognizing that all dialects are legitimate, and we might want to use certain grammatical patterns in certain settings in order to be perceived in the way we want.

In the example above, the focus on practicing intercultural communication skills helped to empower learners to use English in their own ways within different contexts, affirming their abilities to communicate in situations of intercultural interaction or conflict. With the further reflection on non-standard Englishes, I was able to model skills for approaching cultural differences with curiosity and interest rather than judgment.

ISSUES: FRAME THEMES, TOPICS, AND MATERIALS WITH A PEACE PERSPECTIVE

With any curriculum, content can be framed in ways that may help learners not only to think about peace-related issues, but to experience opportunities for transformation through engaging the content. The first step in framing content with a peace perspective is to connect themes and topics to learners' identities and cultures in order for them to bring their full selves into learning. When learners are fully present and engaged with the content, opportunities can arise for the kinds of experiences and dialogues which lead to peacebuilding and reconciliation. Questions to ask about the content include:

- How does the content connect with peacebuilding or reconciliation themes? In what content areas can I bring my knowledge and experience with peacebuilding and reconciliation?
- What different perspectives are presented in the content? Are there voices missing from the topic that need to be added? What additional information can the students or I add to show multiple perspectives and points of view?
- How does the content connect with students' personal and collective identities, worldviews, and cultures? How can I bridge any gaps that exist?

Answers to these questions will help teachers highlight certain aspects of the topic, broaden the topic to include more diverse perspectives, or ask additional questions to prompt further reflection from a peace perspective.

To demonstrate these questions applied to an existing curriculum, I (Cheryl) will use an example from a low intermediate English conversation class for adults in South Korea. The students all wanted to use English in their workplaces with other non-native English speakers and occasionally a visitor from the United States. The curriculum resources and materials I was assigned to use in the class were designed for English language learners residing in the United States in an ESL context. In addition to the problem of using an ESL text in an EFL context, much of the content was a challenge to adapt because it did not contain any themes that could be easily connected to peacebuilding or reconciliation. The perspectives offered by the curriculum were also limited. The textbook tended to describe the culture of white, upper-middle class, English-speaking Americans as "American culture" and did not include any of the many diverse cultures, languages, and people groups that are also part of the United States. The content was also far from my students in terms of their identities. Few of them had ever talked to an English speaker from the United States, let alone visited the places described in the text. Their Korean worldviews also tended to be more collectivist, so the individualist worldview that came through the materials was hard for them to relate to.

In one lesson, we were learning about celebrating American holidays such as Thanksgiving. One connection I found to peacebuilding themes in the text was about nurturing family relationships during the holidays. This resonated with the students, who could then talk about their families and describe them to each other and ask, "What do you do with your family during holidays?" We also added some discussion related to family conflict by asking "What do you talk about with your family on holidays?" and "What do you NOT talk about with your family on holidays?" and compared this to what the article in the textbook suggested about taboo topics in US families. Finally, in talking of Thanksgiving in the United States, the textbook only briefly mentioned Native Americans as part of the original story of the holiday. I modified the language in a short article which introduced a different perspective on the first American settlers' arrival and experience from a Native American point of view. Although we could not discuss the topic to its depth in English only, the Korean students quickly identified with the Native American perspective as the "colonized," given their historical experience of colonization under Japan. The group shared some of their deeper thoughts in a mix of Korean and English, which gave an opportunity for learning a few new words and phrases in English that were not from the text.

In the situation above, I attempted to frame the topics and materials from a peacebuilding perspective by bridging gaps between the content and the learners and by adding multiple perspectives on the stories told. This gave students an opportunity to reflect with new empathy not only on conflict in family contexts but also on the global issue of indigenous rights.

RELATIONSHIPS: CONTINUALLY MONITOR AND PRIORITIZE RELATIONSHIPS

When adapting curricula, teachers can always focus on relationships, even when the lesson objectives, assessments, and student materials are all prescribed. Even with little flexibility, the approaches described in chapter 7 of paying attention to classroom relationships and prioritizing relationships in decision making can work well in any curriculum. According to Tony Jenkin's (n.d.) "Pedagogy of Relationships" framework for peace education, all learning is about relationships: the relationships of student to teacher, of student to self, of student to existing knowledge, of student to emergent knowledge, of student to others, and of student to society. While it may seem like a stretch to think of relationships to knowledge or to self as part of reconciliation, these relationships strongly influence how learners see themselves and thus how they relate to the teacher, others, and society. In adapting a curriculum, sometimes shifting the way students interact with the new knowledge can create opportunities for transforming their relationships in the classroom or the larger society. Questions to ask about the curriculum or materials include:

- How does the curriculum set up the relationship between the students and the teacher? Are there opportunities for connecting deeply and developing both trust and vulnerability? How can I help to create these opportunities within the given curriculum?
- To what extent does the curriculum provide spaces for self-reflection to consider relationships with others, such as self-assessments for group activities? Could this type of reflection be highlighted in or added to existing pair or group tasks?
- How does the curriculum set up students to relate to the new knowledge? What kinds of relationships does this

promote in the classroom or broader society? For example, if students are encouraged to experiment with language and make English their own, they will more likely engage in relationship building using English with others rather than focusing only on using English as a transactional language.

Answers to these questions help teachers focus on the relationships in the classroom and how students are interacting with the language they are learning, which affects their relationships with others and society. This creates an opportunity for nurturing peace and reconciliation in every aspect of classroom interaction.

Consider an advanced English class for immigrant and refugee adults in a small city in Canada. The curriculum is set and the unit is about writing résumés. The curriculum sets up the relationship between students and teachers as the expert teacher and the job-seeking students. The teacher is prompted to answer student questions based on information about résumés from the textbook. The only intentional reflection prompted is for students to consider what "hard" skills and "soft" skills they have that could be added to their résumés, but the teacher's guide says nothing about engaging the learners in group work or relational communication. Based on the introductory materials, the curriculum seems to expect that all students have a direct need to write a résumé and have not written résumés before.

When I (Cheryl) taught this class, I found that the adult learners in the group had a lot of practice with résumé writing in multiple cultures. As we got to know each other, I learned that they had rich vocational and academic experience that actually could add to what the curriculum offered and definitely surpassed my knowledge of the job search world in Canada! So, right away it was easy to redefine our relationship from expert teacher and job-seeking students to inquiring teacher and reflective students. We began the unit by sharing in groups about our experiences with writing résumés, hiring staff based on résumés, and writing about ourselves for other employment or academic purposes. Group members asked questions and affirmed one another during the sharing.

We summarized our experiences with résumés and résumé-like writing on the board, which resulted in a sense of collective pride in all our achievements. Instead of beginning our unit on résumés from a deficit perspective, the learners began with a sense of confidence in their own knowledge and way of doing things, which helped them to engage actively with others in the class. Learners then worked in pairs to look at the materials provided by the curriculum and elicit what was similar and what was different from their experiences. They reflected on what cultural differences these shifts might suggest, learning about each other more deeply. For example, one student suggested that the need to highlight one's achievements in Canadian résumés, which could be considered bragging in another cultural context, reflected the Canadian culture of speaking openly and directly. Finally, students worked in groups to create either their own résumé or one of a fictional character as they chose. They then coached each other on how to improve the résumé before creating mock interviews in which one group had to choose whom to hire from the other group. To wrap up, students completed a self-assessment about how they had worked with their group, reflecting on the relationships that had been built through the activities in the unit.

By creating opportunities for this intentional reflection and shifting the relationship between teachers and students, the group was empowered in their context and affirmed in their abilities and skills to relate in positive ways to others in society. This was significant in a place where immigrants and refugees were often assumed to be inexperienced and uneducated because of their accents or language levels when speaking English. Our efforts of relationship-building in our class empowered learners to relate in positive ways and with confidence when interacting with others in the community, despite the possible discrimination they might face in society. This focus on relationships at the center of reconciliation work can be an opportunity to empower learners for peacebuilding and reconciliation beyond the boundaries of the classroom.

Practical Application: Teaching for Reconciliation with Any Curriculum

1. *Remember the basics.* Keep in mind the students' needs and the purpose of the class. Always maintain transparency with the students in your peacebuilding efforts and involve them whenever possible. Give attention to building peace with co-workers and administration as part of integrating peace-building in your class.
2. *Consider the framework.* Use the framework suggested above to consider aspects of curriculum that you might be able to adapt. Depending on your context, there might be limitations for some, but possibilities in other areas.
3. *Do what you can.* Even if there are too many constraints to adapt the curriculum as you would like, small steps can sometimes shape the class significantly. Don't give up! Keep reflecting on the guiding questions with each new unit and lesson.
4. *Collaborate with colleagues whenever possible.* Peace education is a collaborative effort. Communicate with and educate others in your work place to see if there might be room for changes in the curriculum in the long term or for extracurricular activities like a *Peace Club* or *Sustained dialogue gathering* (see Appendix A for details).

Conclusion

With the group of students applying to be flight attendants, I (Cheryl) was able to adapt the given course a bit in each of the aspects of the Reconciliatory English Teaching Framework. Although the larger purpose of the class was high achievement on a test, which created a context of competition and stress, this intense focus also led to strong engagement from learners. We used interactive and collaborative methodologies for learning, and the speaking and listening skills we practiced lent themselves well to developing intercultural communication skills, which was also an interest for the students as part of their end goal. Because the content was not specified as clearly, we had flexibility to ask questions and go deeper with the speaking prompts in the textbook. Prioritizing relationships led to students interacting in new ways, not only during the class, but also when they met their former classmates as competitors after the course was done. Overall, these small changes and shifts to an otherwise uninspiring and tedious test preparation course transformed all of our experiences in the class. Teaching for reconciliation in settings like this where curriculum is not designed with reconciliatory goals in mind can be a challenging task requiring creative responses to each unique group of students. We may not see the direct outcome of our peacebuilding work, but we are creating the opportunity for reconciliation to happen by nurturing the soil and planting seeds.

CHAPTER 9

SUGGESTIONS FOR DIVERSE SETTINGS AND GOALS

INTRODUCTION

Though many different English teaching and learning contexts have been addressed throughout this book, in this final chapter we look specifically at contextual differences, and how these may impact reconciliatory work within the classroom. We begin by looking at numerous factors which can make one context different from another.

AGE OF LEARNERS

English is learned around the world by individuals of all ages. Learner age influences the selection of methods, materials, and content as we screen for developmental and motivational appropriateness. The language learning process can be quite similar across age groups, but providing an optimal learning environment will look different. For example, older (teen and adult) learners generally bring more prior learning, linguistic understanding, and capabilities for complex abstract thinking which can support the learning process. Older learners may also be highly motivated with well-developed goals of learning English to increase study and job opportunities.

LANGUAGE LEVEL

Language proficiency level is also a significant difference between language learners. For example, beginning language learners cannot engage in "discussion" tasks (unless using the native language) as intermediate and advanced learners can. This does not mean that reconciliatory work cannot be done, but it does mean that it will either be more simplistic and/or nonverbal, or that students will use their native language for parts of the class.

NATIVE LANGUAGES

Another significant factor in an English learning classroom is the native language: whether all students share the same native language, or a common language, and also whether the teacher speaks this language. This is an especially important factor in beginning language classes. If the native language is held in common and can provide a means for extending dialogue into more complex topics, that provides possibilities that do not exist in a class of beginners where there are many different native languages and where, perhaps, the teacher does not speak any of them.

GEOGRAPHICAL LOCATION

In ESL settings, English is spoken among the general population. This means there may be opportunities to use the English language outside of the classroom and build relationships with others who speak English. In EFL settings, English is not a dominant language and is learned and used primarily in school settings. However, the distinction between these two contexts is not black and white in many places. Indonesia, for example, would be considered an EFL context. However, there are many English immersion or bilingual schools in which the school community language is English. Parents who speak English may use a lot of English in the home.

TYPE OF INSTITUTION OR PROGRAM

Children may be learning English in a regular K–12 school setting, either as a foreign language or through content-learning, as in bilingual or full immersion programs. Or, they may be attending an "English school" for after-school English classes. Adults in EFL settings may be learning English in an English school or in university programs. Immigrants in English-speaking countries may be learning English in government-sponsored programs, in church-based programs, or in their place of employment. International students in colleges and universities may be enrolled in intensive English programs or special "bridge" classes in which they continue to learn English while also taking academic classes. Added to these contexts is the learning of English through special programs like English camps. Each of these contexts will provide different opportunities for integrating reconciliation into English learning.

OWNERSHIP OF PROGRAM OR COURSE

A contextual aspect to consider is the "ownership" of the program or course. I (Jan) have distinguished between *host* and *ambassador* contexts (Dormer 2011). When we "own" a school, course, or program, we are the "hosts." We have the freedom to set policies, choose materials, and pursue specific goals. We should be fully transparent in presenting potential learners with what we have to offer, but if we do this, we can design our program in specific ways to be very intentional about teaching English for reconciliation. However, if we are working in a school or program owned by the government, a different religious group, or a business, we are "ambassadors" to that entity. We should first and foremost seek to understand this context and faithfully provide the service that we are contracted to provide. As trust is built, there is often openness to infuse teaching with reconciliatory methods and concepts, perhaps sparking new ideas which can spread beyond the English class.

MINISTRY GOALS

Finally, Christian English language teachers and/or Christian organizations such as mission agencies and churches may have specific ministry goals attached to their teaching of English. Missional goals in English teaching have been addressed in books such as *English Teaching as Christian Mission* (Snow 2001) and *Teaching English in Missions: Effectiveness and Integrity* (Dormer 2011). These texts, and others, emphasize the need for transparency in all missional English teaching efforts, while prioritizing meeting students' needs. If we do not deliver on our promise that our students will learn English by coming to our English classes, then we have no right to offer them anything else. This applies to all Christian-related efforts, such as church-based programs, English camps overseas, and the purposeful placement of English teachers in universities and schools in order to engage in ministry.

As we engage in honest, effective English teaching, we may also have other opportunities to share our Christian faith. This may be an unspoken, lived out faith where students see that we are different in some way and ask us questions, which open doors for sharing our faith. Or, we may be working in contexts where we can use, and transparently state that we use, Christian materials. In these contexts, students may come to our program because they want a Christian English course, or perhaps they have no opinion about the Christian materials, but view the course as a good opportunity to practice their English. Whatever the English ministry context, reconciliatory goals are appropriate.

INTEGRATION OF DIFFERENTIATING FACTORS WITH THE RECONCILIATORY ENGLISH TEACHING FRAMEWORK

We have looked at seven factors of English language teaching contexts that make them different from one another: age of learners, language level, native languages, geographical location, type of institution, ownership of program or course, and ministry goals. We conclude this book by looking at each of these factors through the lens of our Reconciliatory English Teaching Framework. We hope that the following pages will serve as a quick reference tool when questions arise about the applicability of a framework element in a particular context.

While these tables are helpful for keeping in mind just a few of the considerations of each factor and its influence on teaching English for reconciliation, each teaching setting ultimately needs its own analysis, as well as ongoing reassessment as the course is implemented. While assessment of students' language learning is a given for an English class, evaluating reconciliatory goals is relatively new, even in peace education. However, there is a growing body of literature on monitoring and evaluating peacebuilding and peace education, including some practical tools that might be adapted to language classrooms from peacebuilding fields (Del Felice, Karako, and Wisler 2015; Schirch 2013; Search for Common Ground 2016). Adapting some of these tools to the English language teaching context would be one way to explore assessment of reconciliatory goals more deeply.

Tables: Integration of differentiating factors with the Reconciliatory English Teaching Framework

Age of Learners	
Systems: Know the context and where you fit	When teaching children, it is important to understand and respect the school systems involved. When teaching older learners, knowing government or other institutional systems can be helpful in terms of assisting students in navigating and finding their place within those systems.
Methodologies: Choose approaches, groupings, and activities to increase collaboration and empower learners	Many methodologies are appropriate for all age groups. In fact, a common error in thinking is that using manipulatives and moving around during a class period are things that only children enjoy. Where language learning is concerned, adults benefit from most of the same methodologies with an added recognition of their life and learning experience. Adults also benefit from a greater level of choice in activities and clear rationale for why and how a task will be used.
Skills: Model and teach skills to enhance conflict resolution and intercultural communication	Relational skills correlate to emotional maturity, and therefore the types of reconciliatory skills we seek to foster in the language classroom will be somewhat contingent on age. Still, even young children can develop communication patterns that are respectful and that value "hearing" the other person.
Issues: Frame themes, topics, and materials with a peace perspective	The selection of issues may be quite different for students of different ages. Young children think in very concrete terms, and therefore might enjoy a topic such as recycling or helping a neighbor with a cleaning project. Teens are very relational, and hence might engage well with topics connected to insider and outsider groups. Adults have very diverse language-learning purposes, and it is important to select themes and topics which are relevant to them.
Relationships: Continually monitor and prioritize relationships	Young children can learn how to develop positive relationships through language that affirms and values others, and through behaviors such as listening well. Teens are naturally very conscious of relationships, but may not have well developed relational skills. Adults may not have experienced classroom environments that make relationships a priority and may need to grow into this understanding. At all ages, positive classroom relationships are very helpful for both language learning and peacebuilding.

Language level	
Systems: Know the context and where you fit	Students at different language levels require different instruction, and different classroom experiences. One common structural inequity is failure to provide English learning opportunities at the correct language level in order to facilitate acquisition. Teachers may be in a position to speak into larger systems to help address this inequity
Methodologies: Choose approaches, groupings, and activities to increase collaboration and empower learners	Students at different language levels require methodologies that are well-suited for their levels. Teachers should use different kinds of teacher talk, pair, and group experiences and corrective feedback, depending on student levels. That said, students at all language levels benefit from collaboration and activities that empower them as learners.
Skills: Model and teach skills to enhance conflict resolution and intercultural communication	Students at intermediate and advanced language levels are able to engage well in conflict resolution and peacebuilding tasks in English, growing in language and reconciliatory skills as they do so. Students at lower language levels can develop skills in using language at the phrase and sentence level for the purposes of negotiating meaning and clarifying, and relate these to reconciliatory skills they have in other languages.
Issues: Frame themes, topics, and materials with a peace perspective	Some issues utilize more complex language than others. A topic such as the causes of war might be very difficult to pursue with beginning language learners, but might be quite fruitful with advanced learners. Beginners might do well with a theme of friendship, and may be able to engage well in topics such as cyber friendships and having friends in other cultures. All materials used need to be appropriate for the language level of the learners.
Relationships: Continually monitor and prioritize relationships	English learners at all levels need and want good relationships, and limitations in language need not limit the ability to form good relationships. When students are beginners in English, and when they share native languages in common, it is important to allow students to use their native languages to form relationships with classmates. Careful selection of methodologies can help learners at all language levels to build relationships with each other through the English-learning activities.

Native languages	
Systems: Know the context and where you fit	It is helpful to consider the language backgrounds of the students and what influence their linguistic identities may have on their learning. Considering the relationship between their language and English can help teachers to empower students in working with both languages, rather than excluding their other languages from the English learning space
Methodologies: Choose approaches, groupings, and activities to increase collaboration and empower learners	Communicative, task-based, and content-based approaches and REAL activities can be used regardless of students' native languages. Depending on student cultures, some may connect better with certain methodologies than others. Students coming from educational settings that usually use teacher-centered approaches, for example, may benefit from including some more familiar activities as well as more learner-centered ones.
Skills: Model and teach skills to enhance conflict resolution and intercultural communication	When practicing reconciliatory skills, it's helpful to have students compare the skills they are learning in English to their own languages. They may be able to brainstorm ways of communicating well in their own languages. If a common language is shared, they may be able to transfer and translate some of these skills to English together. If students have different languages, they could observe or research in their own languages to share with the class.
Issues: Frame themes, topics, and materials with a peace perspective	When groups have different native languages, talking about the differences in language can be a topic in itself. Reflecting and sharing about their other languages can help students connect better with English structure and grammar. Students can also gather information on different peace issues in their own languages and use their writing to highlight ideas in English that might not be available to English-only readers.
Relationships: Continually monitor and prioritize relationships	Use of native languages strategically in class can help to build relationships. If a group all has the same native language, assigning certain group activities to be discussed in their language first before summarizing in English can build understanding between students. In a class with two or more each of different native languages, grouping people in similar native languages to start a discussion, then moving to mixed language groups to share ideas in English can reinforce positive relationships and help students to get to know each other better.

Geographical location	
Systems: Know the context and where you fit	In an EFL setting, understanding the role of English in the society, general feelings towards the English language, and how students will use English in their lives will be important. For ESL contexts, knowing the challenges students face and what supports might be available to them will help teachers assist them both in and out of the class.
Methodologies: Choose approaches, groupings, and activities to increase collaboration and empower learners	For students in ESL settings, methodologies can include activities which prompt learners to observe and connect with people outside of class. Since many interactions outside of the class will be in English, it is important to use class time to equip students for the tasks they will need to do in their lives. For EFL settings, the classroom may be the only place to practice and use the language regularly. Maximizing student opportunities to communicate directly can happen through activities like role-plays.
Skills: Model and teach skills to enhance conflict resolution and intercultural communication	Students in ESL settings may already be practicing their intercultural communication skills on a daily basis outside of the classroom. Recognizing this in class and helping students to reflect on what works and what doesn't can help to provide support for the kinds of reconciliatory skills they need. In EFL contexts, teachers can ensure that the skills practiced in class match students' contextual and cultural needs and find ways to extend the skills learned in English to their languages and settings outside of class.
Issues: Frame themes, topics, and materials with a peace perspective	Topics and themes for EFL students can vary widely. Often, students are interested in global issues and world events and benefit from opportunities to discuss and write on these topics from their perspectives. For ESL students, daily activities and life events in their communities may provide language or cultural challenges that can be a source for themes and topics. Sharing previous experiences can be a way to connect, but may also require caution if people would rather not talk about their past in class.
Relationships: Continually monitor and prioritize relationships	Relationships are a priority in both EFL and ESL settings. In EFL settings, students likely have extensive communities and friendships. Prompting students to build strong relationships with other students can be one way to prioritize relationships. In an ESL setting, relationships within the new society may not be as easy, as there may be misunderstandings or even discrimination. Relationships with the teacher and in the classroom can empower learners to build stronger relationships with the people they encounter in the broader society.

Type of institution	
Systems: Know the context and where you fit	Different types of institutions may offer support or restrictions in working for reconciliatory goals. In a K–12 setting, there may be additional opportunities outside of class to collaborate on whole school approaches to peacebuilding. In university settings, working with other students on campus may be possible. Private English schools may differ considerably from each other, depending on the level of prescriptiveness in their systems. Thinking of the institution's supporters and larger constituency can help to frame reconciliatory goals.
Methodologies: Choose approaches, groupings, and activities to increase collaboration and empower learners	The type of institution may influence the kinds of methodologies teachers choose to use. In more formal educational settings, there may be limits to the space or time available for certain activities or projects. In a church or community-based program, there may be more flexibility. In most institutions, there is support for meeting the learners' needs, and when the stated need is developing English language proficiency, a strong case can be made for using learner-focused methodologies.
Skills: Model and teach skills to enhance conflict resolution and intercultural communication	Within any institution, conflict resolution and intercultural communication skills would be relevant for students. The type of institution, though, could affect which skills to focus on. In a university setting, skills for working with professors and supervisors would be helpful. For adults coming to an evening class after work, leadership skills and conflict management for the workplace might be helpful. Children in K–12 settings may focus more on skills for solving problems with family and classmates.
Issues: Frame themes, topics, and materials with a peace perspective	When working with more formal educational settings, themes and topics may be restricted to align with larger curriculum objectives for other courses. There may be more flexibility in short-term programs or community-supported classes. Likewise, government-funded programs may have specific expectations of topics and themes to address in the class. If so, the suggestions outlined in chapter 8 may be useful.
Relationships: Continually monitor and prioritize relationships	Relationships are central in any type of institution. The nature of relationships and which relationships are the focus may shift between formal and informal settings. Many teachers in K–12 settings will meet students repeatedly as they move through the grades. This provides a unique opportunity for getting to know students on a deeper level. In other settings, the time together may be quite short or there may be a lot of turn-over in student enrollment, which can provide challenges for building deeper relationships.

Ownership of program or course (Host or Ambassador orientation)	
Systems: Know the context and where you fit	While there are always some external systems such as governments which may exert an influence over students and programs, if a teacher belongs to the organization that owns the English program or course, she or he has much more flexibility over the inclusion of reconciliatory objectives.
Methodologies: Choose approaches, groupings, and activities to increase collaboration and empower learners	Ownership of a program, school, or course usually means full freedom to select the methodologies that teachers feel are appropriate for the learners. In this case, the ideas in chapter 7 are very relevant. If the teacher is not a part of the organization that owns the program or course, the ideas in chapter 8 can help to focus on the reconciliatory methodologies that are possible.
Skills: Model and teach skills to enhance conflict resolution and intercultural communication	Skills to enhance conflict resolution and intercultural communication are likely to be valued in all programs. If part of the controlling organization, the teacher may be able to emphasize these skills more, but even where the teacher is an *ambassador* to another program, such skills foster overall communicative ability, and therefore are frequently seen as valuable.
Issues: Frame themes, topics, and materials with a peace perspective	Teachers may have a great deal of choice in the selection of themes and topics when working in a *host* context, within a program that the teacher's organization owns. If the program is run by someone else, it is important to prioritize achieving the stated goals. Within those goals, however, there is often some latitude in selecting topics used to develop the various language skills, and it is often possible to allow students to take stated themes and topics in directions which interest them and which meet particular needs.
Relationships: Continually monitor and prioritize relationships	Relationships are important, no matter who owns the program. The *host* teacher may have full discretion to create curricula and lessons which place relationships at center stage in the classroom. If teachers are *ambassadors* to another program or course, they must first pay attention to their own relationship to the owners or directors of that course, modeling a good relationship at the leadership level. This helps to establish a culture that emphasizes relating well in any situation.

Ministry goals	
Systems: Know the context and where you fit	External systems may have a significant impact on what kinds of ministry goals are possible or advisable. Some governments or communities may not welcome English classes in which students are learning about the Bible or Christianity, and other contexts may view this as the learner's choice. It is always important to know and respect local systems and to be transparent and authentic in our goals.
Methodologies: Choose approaches, groupings, and activities to increase collaboration and empower learners	Methodologies selected for reconciliatory goals work very well with ministry goals. Whether ministry goals involve being "salt and light" without explicit mention of the gospel, or whether discussions of Christianity can freely occur for more evangelistic or discipleship goals, the methodologies in chapters 7 and 8 and in the appendices will work well because they affirm and focus on the learner.
Skills: Model and teach skills to enhance conflict resolution and intercultural communication	The skill set of a reconciliatory teacher, as described in this book, should be a requirement for all English-teaching ministries! Likewise, fostering skills in students of reflection, recognition of other ways of thinking, and engaging in respectful and productive conversations will only enhance a learner's potential to hear and consider discussions of Christianity.
Issues: Frame themes, topics, and materials with a peace perspective	We have talked throughout this book about the selection of peace-related themes and topics. These are very relevant to ministry endeavors, as the pursuit of reconciliation is a Christian value. In contexts where religion can be openly discussed, some peace themes could be mediated via biblical texts, such as the parable of the Good Samaritan. Teachers engaged in teaching English in ministry should know the limitations or possibilities of their given context, but not be afraid to utilize the Bible and Christian materials where this kind of content is permissible and meets the students' language learning needs.
Relationships: Continually monitor and prioritize relationships	If we want our students to learn about God and the reconciliation to himself that is offered through Jesus Christ, we need to first model positive, identity-affirming, life-promoting relationships with our students. As we model this way of relating to others, we may then be in a position to share about our relationship to Jesus Christ or to help those who are believers grow in their relationship to him.

CONCLUSION

This book has looked at the "why," "who," and "how" of teaching English for reconciliation in a variety of contexts. Drawing on knowledge and resources from the rich fields of peacebuilding and peace education, English language teachers can know that we are not alone in engaging in the "ministry of reconciliation." While the connections between language learning and reconciliation are still being explored, we have experienced these connections first-hand as teachers and know that there are incredible possibilities for students and teachers to transform their relationships in the classroom, their communities, and beyond. The identities and cultures of learners in their unique contexts shape not only how language learning happens, but also how opportunities for reconciliation might occur through language learning. In the midst of this dynamic space of the classroom community, teachers also bring in their identities, characteristics, and dispositions that can help increase these possibilities for building peace. Whether teachers have much flexibility or little choice in curriculum design and implementation, considering the unique aspects of each teaching context plays a key role in applying the strategies suggested in this book.

We hope that other Christian English language teachers who desire to be involved in the "ministry of reconciliation" (2 Cor 5:18, NIV) and to "seek peace and pursue it" (Ps 34:14, NIV) have been inspired through the stories and suggestions throughout these pages. We wish you God's guidance and inspiration as you pursue peace through transformed relationships in your language learning and teaching context.

Appendix A

Suggested Activities

1. Group-up (Ch. 5)

This whole class activity can be used as an icebreaker or as any task to find out what the group has in common. An open-ended question (i.e., without a "right" or "wrong" answer) is called out such as "What is your favorite color? Group up!" and students have to talk to each other in order to gather together with people who have a similar answer. After clusters have formed around the room, the facilitator can ask each group what their answer is. This can be a helpful activity to recognize voices on the margins that differ from the mainstream. If one person has a unique answer that does not fit in any group, facilitators should affirm their responses and try to find what wisdom their answer has for the group.

2. Total Physical Response (TPR) (Ch. 5)

This whole class activity can be used as an opening activity when introducing a unit or a lesson, or to provide an active break between sedentary activities. Basically, it is the process of one person making a statement that invites everyone else to respond with a physical action instead of a verbal one. In beginning language levels, it could be as simple as the teacher calling out and modeling "stand up," "sit down," "turn around," and similar phrases. After modeling the first time, the teacher should refrain from performing the action, so that students can demonstrate their understanding of the language. Also, at the beginning students should not be required to speak. TPR is an excellent activity for beginning language learners precisely because it does not force students to speak. However, if there are students in the class who are eager to talk, students can take over the teacher's role of calling out commands, thus gaining some practice in speaking as well.

At intermediate or advanced language levels, commands or statements can be tied more specifically to content, such as "Raise your hand (or stand up) if you use Facebook," to introduce a session on cyber friendships. A follow-up could be asking students to show how often they check Facebook by holding up five fingers for several times a day to one finger for once a week or less (write this scale on the board). At high intermediate or advanced language proficiency levels, the teacher can write or speak a statement with which students could agree or disagree without judgment, such as "Students should wear uniforms in schools," to introduce a topic of schools and bullying, then ask students to line up based on how strongly they agree with the statement. Students might then discuss why they stood where they did along the line.

3. I AM FROM . . . (CH. 5)

This writing exercise is based on George Ella Lyon's (2016) poetry writing prompt. Create a list of different categories of items related to a person's culture and identity such as "a family tradition," "a phrase you heard often as a child," "a family food," or "description of a place you went often as a child." Ask students to write their lists first. Then students add "I am from . . ." before each item and add the lines together to complete the poem. This activity can be adapted to use categories appropriate for the context.

4. CONCENTRIC CIRCLES (CH. 5)

This is a whole class activity that is a helpful way for students to practice speaking about the same topic to different partners. It requires two equally-sized groups of at least three or more students. One group stands in a circle facing out. The other group stands in an outer circle facing in around the inner circle. As a result, students are paired facing another student. After engaging in discussion about the topic for a set amount of time, the outer circle moves clockwise one person and the students can discuss again with a new partner. After the time elapses again, the inner circle moves counter clockwise and students can discuss again. This process repeats until everyone has discussed with everyone else or the total time for the activity has ended. This activity can also be done in lines rather than circles. This may spread the students out more, and make the classroom less noisy!

5. VOCABULARY PARTNERS (CH. 5)

This is an activity that is best used as a regular ritual over several classes or a whole term. Students are paired with another person in class for the first session. While strategic pairing is ideal for this activity, random pairing can also work, depending on the context. Students are given time each class to work together on a vocabulary-related task, such as identifying words they are not familiar with in a reading and discerning meaning from context, or finding academic synonyms for common words in their own writing. It is usually helpful to have the same task each time the partners meet so that they can focus on completing the task rather than understanding instructions. The goal is for students to talk together to try to figure out their own understandings with the resources they have before turning to the teacher for answers. This also is a helpful way to build relationships because a student can get to know one other student more deeply and students can support each other.

6. GROUP DUTIES (CH. 5)

This activity works well prior to any type of group task, as it entails understanding the roles that need to be fulfilled by members of the group. Depending on the students' language proficiency level, the teacher or the students prepare a list of different roles that are needed in order to complete the required task, such as "discussion leader," "note-taker," "turn-taking monitor," "questioner," "time keeper," "summary presenter," or other roles. Then each group decides who will do each role. Optionally, the group could take turns and try out different roles for different parts of a discussion task. This activity is helpful to ensure that each group member is valued and included in the group task.

7. CARD SORTS (CH. 5)

This group activity is based on a task used for group decision making or problem solving (Kraybill and Wright 2007). Students are given an open-ended question, such as "What ways do you enjoy learning?" or a problem to solve, such as "How can we make our school a happier place?" Then students write their answers or ideas on sticky notes, one idea or answer per note. After a set time for writing, the group silently posts their notes on the board or a spot on the wall so others in the group can also read the ideas. Students are instructed not to talk or discuss, just to read the other notes and ask only questions for clarifying understanding if needed. After everyone in the group has read the notes, they categorize the cards either silently with a final discussion at the end (beginner–intermediate), or with discussion throughout (advanced). Criteria for categorization will emerge from the group and there will often, but not always, be a consensus at some point about the categorization. Finally, the group can present to the whole class the results of their ideas or answers based on categories. With more advanced language proficiency, debriefing the experience of the process can also be a way to build awareness of group decision-making processes and group dynamics.

8. MAINSTREAMS AND MARGINS (CH. 5)

This whole class activity for high-intermediate to advanced language proficiency learners is modified from an adult learning task designed to bring awareness of mainstream and margin dynamics in a group (Lakey 2010). In the English language class, this can be an exercise to introduce a topic that requires some empathy, related to marginalized voices. Begin with asking students to reflect silently on a time they felt left out, excluded, or on the margins. They do not need to share their story with others; just share how they felt when in that situation. Draw a large circle on the board and write the feelings that students share just outside the circle. Then ask students to reflect on characteristics of the group that would be considered "in" or "mainstream" in their situation, in essence, the characteristics of the group doing the excluding. When students share, write those characteristics on the inside of the circle. Then draw arrows from the inside of the circle to the outside and ask them to brainstorm, "What could the people on the inside do to have a better relationship with the people on the outside?" Write ideas on the board. At this point, depending on the context, teachers may want to elicit how the students might understand a different perspective by reflecting on their experiences in this exercise. Alternatively, students can be asked to think about situations or times they might be more in the inside group and share anything they might be able to do to understand the outside group in those situations. Affirm any attempts that students make at understanding another perspective.

9. MORE AND LESS (CH. 5)

This is a whole class activity for prompting reflection on marginalization and building empathy and is best done with young adult or adult learners at any language proficiency level. The teacher prepares enough of a simple item such as stickers, pebbles, or colored slips of paper to distribute to five times the number in the class. Students sit in a circle and the teacher randomly hands out an uneven number of the items to each person. Some get one item, others get seven or ten, others get two, and a few get several times that of everyone else. After distributing them, ask students to reflect on how they feel. Provide feeling vocabulary (e.g., "left out," "ashamed," "ignored," "rich," "poor") according to their proficiency level ahead of time as needed. Write "more" and "less" with a line drawn between them like a continuum on the board. Ask one student to share how they feel about the number of items they received. Ask the others whether they think that student has "more" or "less" and write their feeling on the board at the appropriate place on the line. Repeat these questions until there are a number of feelings on the board between "more" and "less." Then, have the students with the most items swap with the students who had the least items and ask again how they feel and write their answers with the others. Finally, ask students to think about a time in their life when they have more or less of something and give an example, such as "more friends" or "less fun" and compare their feeling at the time to the feelings on the board. Depending on the proficiency level of the class, a follow-up could be a deeper discussion or a writing assignment.

10. SONGS (CH. 7)

There are many songs and worksheets online for English language teaching. On my (Jan's) website (https://sites.google.com/site/jandormerspage/), I have a number of freely downloadable audio files of songs with accompanying worksheets, like this one:

LEAN ON ME

"... let us encourage one another ..." (Hebrews 10:25b)

Completion

Lean on Me when _____ not strong
I'll be _____ friend, I'll help you _____ on
For I know, it won't _____ long, till I'm gonna _____
Somebody to lean _____
_____ just call on me _____ when you need a
_____

We all need somebody _____ lean on
I just _____ have a problem that _____ understand
We all need _____ to lean on

Idioms

Match the phrases with the definitions:

to continue	lean on
count on / rely on	call on
ask for help	carry on

Use the idioms to fill in the blanks below.

1. Can I _____ you if I need help?
2. Don't _____ on that fence. It's broken.
3. My job is difficult, but I will _____.

Questions

1. When do you "lean on" others? _____
   _____
2. Can others "lean on" you? How and when? _____
   _____

11. DICTO-COMP (CH. 7)

This combination of dictation and composition (adapted from Wajnryb 1988) can be used successfully for older children and adults. It practices all four skills (reading, writing, speaking, and listening), and helps students develop accuracy in language use. Begin with a short (3–4 sentence) paragraph that is written at the students' language level and that is meaningful to them. The advantage for peacebuilding goals is that you can choose a paragraph which helps further those goals. For example, I chose the paragraph below to help intermediate level learners consider the potential in the simple action of smiling. Where English is concerned, the paragraph also models the use of helping verbs such as can, could, should, might, etc.

> Have you ever thought about the value of a smile? A smile can make those around you feel better. A smile could help to resolve a conflict, even more than the words you say. And smiling at your teacher might even help you get better grades! Of course, a smile should be genuine. But even if you don't feel like smiling, smiling can make you feel better.

After selecting a paragraph, follow these steps:

1. Introduce the topic so that students will be prepared for the text. This could include asking questions, showing pictures, or introducing vocabulary words.
2. Read the paragraph to the students. Do not allow them to write anything down.
3. Read the paragraph again, allowing students to take notes. Repeat this step a few times, if necessary.
4. Ask students to rewrite the paragraph, based on their notes. Give them these guidelines:

   - Their writing should have the same ideas.
   - Their writing should be grammatically correct.

- Their writing does not need to be exactly like the paragraph you read.

5. In groups of 3–4, have students share their paragraphs and come up with a group version.
6. Students write their group versions on the board or on large papers which can be put on the wall.
7. The teacher reads each paragraph as it is completed, under-lining parts that may need work. Groups gather around their versions, correcting them and soliciting the teacher's help as needed.
8. All groups read their paragraphs to the class.

12. SURVEYS (CH. 7)

Surveys are an excellent activity in language classrooms, as they provide the opportunity to ask the same question again and again to different classmates. The teacher provides a table which students fill out as they go around the room asking their class-mates the specified questions. The question and answer prompts are provided on the survey sheet so that students will practice the desired language forms. Surveys are very helpful in language development, especially for beginners. Surveys can also be instru-mental in achieving reconciliatory teaching goals, as they can be very relational. Surveys can have students asking each other questions about likes, dislikes, experiences, beliefs, opinions, and more. In this way, they are a great tool to help classmates get to know one another better. Here is an example:

Q: Do you like _____?

A: Yes, I like   _____ .

No, I don't like   _____ .

Name	bananas	apples	papaya	pineapple
Mario	√	√	X	√

13. INTERVIEWS (CH. 7)

In surveys, students ask the same question to many people. In interviews, they ask different questions to the same person. Thus, interviews can help students develop and use more language, and they can also build relationships at a deeper level. Interviews can be used at all language levels beyond the very beginning. The lower the language level, the more important it is to *guide* the interview task. A guided interview assignment is shown below.

In this task, the teacher first directs students to write their interview questions on the chart. After students have attempted this, the teacher might engage in whole-class instruction to check the questions. Then, students will be paired for the interview, and students will write their partner's answers on their chart. Finally, students will use the guided writing model to write a short paragraph about their partner.

Write about Your Friend!

Ask your friend:

	Question	Answer
Name		
Country		
Age		
Birthday		
Sisters		
Brothers		
Hobbies		

My friend is _____. ____ comes from _____. _____ is ____ years old. _____ birthday is on _____. _____ has ____ sisters and ____ brothers. _____ likes to _____. I like my new _____!

This kind of interview template and process can be changed in many ways, for different language levels and for different purposes. For example, the interviews could focus on where students have lived, cultural differences, or opinions about something the teacher has had students read or view. The possibilities are endless!

14. Find Someone Who . . .

This familiar ice-breaker game also has a lot of potential in the English language classroom. Teachers can create lists that will help to both build relationships and practice English, based on their knowledge of the students in the classroom. Students go around asking their classmates if they can answer "yes" to any of the questions and collecting signatures. This activity can work well at any level, as long as the language used is at the students' level. The sample below might work well for low intermediate levels and above. In this sample, students gain practice paying attention to the presence or absence of "s" on the verb (e.g., "Find someone who writes . . ." changed to "Do you write . . ."). This activity is also excellent for relationship-building as it gets students thinking about the issue of stress and coping mechanisms. When students talk with a partner after the "find someone who" activity, they may be able to share at a deeper level about the stressors they experience.

How do your classmates cope with stress? Find someone who . . .

1. writes in a journal   Name: _____

Question prompt: **Do you . . . ?**

2. talks to a friend   Name: _____
3. talks to a family member   Name: _____
4. eats ice cream   Name: _____
5. goes shopping   Name: _____
6. goes running   Name: _____
7. reads a book   Name: _____
8. other: _____   Name: _____

Write, then talk with a partner:

Do any of your classmates cope with stress in the same way that you do?

_____

Would you like to change how you cope with stress?

_____

Does your partner have any advice for coping with stress?

_____

For lower level classes, students could be asked to find classmates who like different colors, have certain numbers of siblings, have had common health issues like broken bones, go to specific places, like different sports . . . and much more!

15. UPSET THE FRUIT BASKET

This is a well-known circle game that can be adapted for language practice. It is yet another activity which not only helps students practice certain vocabulary or language structures, but which can also help them to get to know each other. The game is played with everyone sitting in a circle (divide into two circles if the class is large), with one person standing in the middle. That person says something which causes others to move. When they move, the person in the middle tries to get one of the seats.

In a beginning class where students have been learning about families, the teacher might provide the prompt, "Move if you . . ." along with some possible sentence endings: "Move if you have a brother" or "Move if you have two grandparents." In a more advanced class, the teacher might set up a prompt like this one, focusing on present perfect:

"I haven't ever _____. Move if you *have.* GO!"

And then switch it to:

"I have _____. Move if you *haven't.* GO!"

It is helpful to present the prompts and have students write down some possibilities before you begin playing the game, as it is difficult to "think on your feet" in a second language. It is also helpful to teach students to wait for the word GO before they move. This allows language learners more time to process the statement and decide whether they need to move or not.

16. CIRCLE PRACTICE

Students and teacher sit in a circle. The teacher begins by speaking a word, phrase, or question to a student next to her. That student repeats it to the next student, and so on. Often an exchange can be practiced, such as the following:

T:	This is an apple (handing the student an apple).
S1:	What?
T:	An apple.
S1:	This is an apple.
S2:	What?
S1:	An apple.
S2:	This is an apple.

And the apple continues around the circle. If this activity is being used for *review* rather than for introducing new content, the teacher may start a second phrase after the first has been done by one or two students. For more fun (and confusion!) start another phrase going in the opposite direction around the circle!

Appendix B

Sample Forms and Plans

Understanding a Teaching Context

Use the following form to collect information about the context prior to teaching a new group of students.

National/Ethnic profiles:

Group 1:

Country: _____ Number of students: M: ___ F: ___
Ethnicities: _____
Native languages: _____
Language levels: _____
Ages: _____
Religion(s): _ _____
Important history: _____

Group 2:

Country: _____ Number of students: M: ___ F: ___
Ethnicities: _____
Native languages: _____
Language levels: _____
Ages: _____
Religion(s): _ _____
Important history: _____

(Repeat for each additional student group.)

Language level profiles:

Level _____   Describe in terms of characteristics above:

_____

_____

_____

Level _____   Describe in terms of characteristics above:

_____

_____

_____

Describe any historical or current tensions between any of the students:

_____

_____

_____

Describe any historical or current tensions between any of the students and the local community:

_____

_____

_____

Describe any historical or current tensions between the teacher's and the students' cultures or countries:

_____

_____

_____

Describe any significant differences between students, which might naturally result in very different perspectives:

_____

_____

_____

Given the conditions described above, describe some areas of potential growth and learning in reconciliation for this class:

1. _____
   _____
   _____

2. _____
   _____
   _____

3. _____
   _____
   _____

Now, transfer these goals to the chart below and add language situations and possible strategies, methods, or materials to achieve goals.

Goals	Language considerations	Possible strategies, methods, or materials to achieve goals

UNIT PLANNING

The following information can help teachers understand how to plan learning units. An explanation of the various components of unit planning is provided first and followed by a sample unit plan.

Reconciliation is hard work. If any progress is to be made toward such goals in an English language classroom, it will likely not take place in one class period. So, it is helpful to first look at planning in terms of *units*—a series of sequential lessons. Following is a description of the parts of a unit plan.

Context: A summary of all the information in "understanding a teaching context" goes here. At the minimum, the context needs to provide this information:

- Age of learners
- Language proficiency level of learners
- Setting/facilities/constraints
- Potential for growth in peacebuilding and reconciliation

Objectives: All instructional planning, at any level, begins with objectives. What is it that you hope the students will learn? More precisely, what do you hope they will be able to *do,* that they could not do before? Where English teaching for reconciliation is concerned, we should actually envision two goals: *peacebuilding objectives* and *language objectives.* Further, we may want to clearly state the overall goal where peacebuilding or reconciliation is concerned.

Topic/theme: In language classes the topic of our class may not be the objective of the class. For example, my language objective might be that students use past tense. But the topic of my lesson will not be "past tense." That would be boring! Instead, the topic might be "childhood memories"—which will require the use of past tense and which also may build relationships as students share about their lives.

Time: How many sessions are in the unit? How many minutes is each session? This information helps you know how much time you have to achieve the objectives. After identifying the time, it might be necessary to return to "objectives" to either broaden or narrow the goals of the unit. Specifically, where peacebuilding goals are concerned, it is important to consider what kinds of objectives might be realistic within a given time frame.

Individual lesson topics and objectives: Your unit plan should provide an overview of what topics and objectives (both language and peacebuilding) will be addressed in each lesson.

Assessment plan: Good teaching is always accompanied by assessment. How will you know if students have achieved the objectives? The answer to this question is your assessment plan! Instruction and assessment need to work hand in hand: you identify what goals you want students to reach, design an assessment plan to evaluate how well the goals have been reached, then design instruction so that students will be able to do well on the assessment. Your peacebuilding goals, as well, should be identified. What progress do you hope to see in peacebuilding, relational interactions, or conflict resolution?

Following is a sample unit plan, illustrating the integration of English learning with peacebuilding goals.

UNIT PLAN: PERSONALITY

Context: An ESL class for refugees in Canada

- Age of learners: adults
- Language proficiency level of learners: intermediate
- Setting/facilities/constraints: Good classroom facilities; white boards, moveable chairs, projector

Peacebuilding goal: Students have come from opposites sides of a war. They need an opportunity to get to know each other on "safe" topics that allow some self-disclosure but do not get into sensitive issues related to the war. It is hoped that the topic of "personality" can provide this safe yet relational interaction.

Objectives:

Peacebuilding objectives:

1. Students will identify shared personality traits.
2. Students will collaborate with others who share basic, inherent qualities rather than ethnic or language allegiances.
3. Students will collaborate with others who have different personality characteristics.

4. Students will articulate values in working with those who are similar and with those who are different.

Language objectives:

1. Students will learn adjectives describing personalities and use these to describe themselves and others in writing and speaking.
2. Students will use agreement phrases: *me too, so do I, I do too*
3. Students will use the verbs *like, don't like, enjoy,* and *love* followed by gerunds and infinitives for first and third person, singular and plural (e.g., I like going . . . ; I don't like to play . . . ; He loves singing . . . ; We enjoy writing . . .)

Topic/theme: Personality types

Time: Six lessons, sixty min. each

Individual lesson topics and objectives:

Lesson	Topic	Reconciliatory Objective Students will . . .	Language Objective Students will . . .
1	Describe your personality	Develop awareness of their own strengths, abilities, and preferences	Identify 15–20 personality adjectives
2	Take a personality test (such as the "Short personality quiz" at Psych Central http://psychcentral.com/quizzes/personality.htm)	Focus on characteristics that are human rather than cultural	Understand the "Big 5" personality characteristics: • extraversion • agreeableness • conscientiousness • emotional stability • openness to experiences Develop reading comprehension
3	Find personality buddies	Identify shared personality traits	Use agreements: *me too, so do I, I do too.*
4	Market your personality!	Collaborate with similar personalities; identify personality strengths	Use affirmative agreements: *me too, so am I, I am too (same using third person)*
5	Use your personality!	Collaborate with different personalities; highlight the value of personality difference	Use *like, don't like, enjoy,* and love followed by gerunds/ infinitives
6	Market your skills!	Work together in a diverse group to sell each others' strengths; write a guided reflection commenting on what has been learned about groupmates and the success of the collaboration.	Demonstrate the ability to use the language above in writing on a poster and orally for a presentation

Assessment of Language Objectives: Students will work in diverse personality groups to identify a group project that they are uniquely suited for. They will then market their team as an expert group. They will create a poster which should showcase various personality traits and their usefulness. They will provide an oral presentation which must include some use of tag endings, gerunds, and infinitives.

Assessment of Peacebuilding Objectives: Students will write a reflection on what has been learned about their groupmates and the success of the collaboration. The teacher will provide key guiding questions which the learners will address in their reflection.

LESSON PLANNING

The following information can help teachers understand how to plan lessons. An explanation of the PPPP lesson planning template is provided first, followed by a sample lesson plan.

After context planning and unit planning, each lesson is elaborated through a lesson plan. It is a good idea to create fairly detailed lesson plans when you are beginning to teach or are beginning to incorporate peacebuilding goals into your lessons. One lesson plan template is the PPPP format:

Prepare:
Introduce the topic; activate students' background knowledge and get them interested; use this short opening activity to assess group dynamics.

Present:
Introduce the new language—usually new words or new grammatical structures; consider how learners can be empowered through the methods used (e.g., introducing new language in a learner-centered way by having learners guess and discover, rather than through a teacher-centered lecture)

Practice:
Provide guided or controlled practice. Practice activities should be directed enough by the teacher at this stage so that students are using the new language correctly, with appropriate corrective feedback from the teacher; plan for ways to give feedback that support and respect learners and help build a positive space.

Perform:
Provide opportunities for students to use the language with less guidance, for real, meaningful, authentic communication. During this phase of the lesson, teachers can engage in informal assessment, checking for accurate student use of the new language and monitoring group dynamics and peacebuilding objectives

There are many other possible lesson plan formats. At the very least, a good lesson plan clearly states the objectives of the lesson and what the teacher and students will say and do in each part of the lesson. A good plan for language learning normally spends only a very brief time introducing new words or grammatical structures and uses the majority of class time to provide students with opportunities to use the new language for meaningful communication and relationship-building.

SAMPLE LESSON PLAN

FIND PERSONALITY BUDDIES

(Lesson #3 in Unit Plan on Personality)

Teacher: Jan Dormer
Lesson Time/Date/Length: Wed., Oct. 5, 9:00–10:00; 60 minutes
Lesson topic: Shared personality traits
Grade/Age: Adult
Language Level: Intermediate
Context: Refugees in Canada
Language Objectives: Students will use agreements: me too, so am I, I am too (same using third person singular and plural)
Reconciliatory Objectives: Students will identify with others through shared personality traits

PREPARE (review; build interest)
Time: 15 min.
Materials: List of personality adjectives from lesson #1, on the board or on a chart.
Activities:

1. Using the personality adjectives learned in lesson #1, play "upset the fruit basket". The person standing in the middle will make a statement following this model: "Move if you are *outgoing*. GO!" Those who are outgoing must move. (See Appendix A for a full description of this game.)

2. Have students work in pairs to review the "big 5" personality traits from lesson #2 (extraversion, agreeableness, conscientiousness, emotional stability, openness to experiences). Have them create sentences about each of the five following this model: "Extraversion means that a person…"

PRESENT (elicit; lead students to discovery)
Time: 10 min.
Teach affirmative agreements as follows:

1. Have students write down five simple "I am" statements about themselves. Provide the following model sentences orally and on the board: I am a person, I am a woman, I am a daughter, I am short, I am usually happy"

2. Have students take turns reading their statements. To each reply:
    Affirmative: So am I / I am too / Me too (alternate these; write them on the board as you say them)
    OR
    Negative: I'm not

3. Have students go around the room saying their statements to each other. Instruct them to respond as you have responded, and to alternate the affirmative responses so that they practice all three.

PRACTICE (controlled, meaningful language use)
Time: 25 min.
Materials: Students' personality test results; Handout: survey on high and low personality traits
Activities:

1. Give students the survey handout. Read through the directions, having them circle the highs and lows on their forms. Have students engage in the survey by finding out if their classmates are the same or different in each category.

2. After surveys have been completed, refer to your own personality test and a student who is the same in one category, making a sentence such as: "I am high in openness to new experiences, and *so is John.*" Write the agreement phrase ("so is John") on the board. Draw attention to the switch from "am" to "is". Elicit this additional form: "John is too".

3. Have each student formulate a statement about themselves and another student who is the same, such as "I am low in extraversion and so is Maria." Have students share aloud, requiring that each student share at least one statement.

4. Extend the language to plural. Using information that students have shared about their personalities, make a model statement such as "I am high in openness to new experiences, and *so are* John, Tran, and Hae Min." and "I am high in openness to new experiences, and John, Tran, and Hae Min *are too.*" Give students a few minutes to write similar statements, using their survey data. Have them share with the class.

PERFORM (performance-based assessment)
Time: 10 min.
Materials: Chart paper, markers
Activities:
Ask students to get in groups of 2-4 with others who are most like them. Students can use all of the information that has been shared aloud, and their survey data. Have them first prepare a chart to present, showing their commonalities in some of the personality traits. Then, have each group tell the rest of the class how their group is alike, by having each person make statements such as this: "I am low in extraversion and so are Paulo and Mohammed."

Handout: Survey on high and low personality traits

Name: _____

Instructions:

1. Look at your personality score. Circle "high" or "low" in each category, to tell about yourself.
2. Go around the room, telling your classmates about yourself. Your classmates will respond with agreement or disagreement. Example:

   You: I am high in extraversion.
   Classmate: So am I / Me too / I am too
   OR
   I am not.

3. Beside each classmates' name, write "S" for "same" or "D" for "different" in each column.

Classmates' names	Extraversion High/low	Agreeableness High/low	Conscientiousness High/low	Emotional stability High/low	Openness to experiences High/low

Appendix C

Resources

English Teaching Resources

- Jan Dormer's webpage: https://sites.google.com/site/jandormerspage/. This is a website of free English-teaching resources. See especially "English Teacher's Helper," which provides many teaching methods, "English to Sing and Learn," which contains audio files for classroom songs, as well as a workbook with materials for each of the songs, and "English for Life," a five-level task-based curriculum.
- Two books by I.S.P. Nation:
  o Nation, I.S.P. and Newton, Jonathan (2008) *Teaching ESL/EFL Listening and Speaking* (ESL & Applied Linguistics Professional Series). New York, NY: Routledge. ISBN-13: 978-0415989701
  o Nation, I.S.P. (2008) *Teaching ESL/EFL Reading and Writing* (ESL & Applied Linguistics Professional Series). New York, NY: Routledge. ISBN-13: 978-0415989688
  These books provide an excellent overview of the skills of listening, speaking, reading, and writing, along with an abundance of methods and materials for developing these skills.
- This book by Amy Buttner Zimmer is chock full of engaging methods for the language classroom.
  o Zimmer, Amy Buttner (2014). *Activities, Games, and Assessment Strategies for the World Language Classroom.* (2nd ed.) New York, NY: Routledge ISBN: 978-1138827295

- The "Passport to Adventure" EFL (English as a Foreign Language) series for children, produced by Purposeful Design (the publication arm of Association of Christian Schools International) is the only published Christian EFL series of its kind. Information can be found at https://safe. acsi.org/eWeb/DynamicPage.aspx?site=pd&webcode=efl

PEACE EDUCATION MATERIALS

- The Cultivating Peace website has helpful resources as well as links to other peace education materials on peacebuilding, multiculturalism, human rights, and other topics at http:// www.cultivatingpeace.ca/pematerials/online.html.
- The Conflict Resolution in Education website has a wealth of resources as well as this connection of links here: http:// www.creducation.org/cre/global_cre/peace_education_ resources. They also host an international conference for educators which is an excellent opportunity for further learning about peace education and reconciliation.
- This link at the Teach for Peace contains information on several well-used peace education curriculum resources that can be adapted for English language teaching contexts: http://www.teachforpeace.org/rationales-curricula/ Peace-Education-Curricula-Resources.
- Peace.ca website contains an ever-growing list of materials for peace education: http://www.peace.ca/curricula.htm
- Quaker educators have developed a number of helpful peace education resources listed here: http://www.quaker. org.uk/our-work/peace/peace-education
- The Global Campaign for Peace Education has an excellent compilation of materials here: http://www.peace-ed-cam-paign.org/category/categories/curricula/ and send out regular makings with helpful links and peace education resources from around the world.

- Montessori schools have developed many great resources for young learners that can be found here: http://www.montessoriservices.com/community-peace/peace-resources
- For more information on putting together a peace education course, Tony Jenkins's resource *Community-based Institutes on Peace Education Organizer's Manual: A Peace Education Planning Guide* (New York, NY: International Institute on Peace Education, 2007; available online at www.c-i-p-e.org) is a valuable resource.

REFERENCES

Allport, G. W. (1954). *The nature of prejudice.* Cambridge, MA: Addison-Wesley.

Armster, M. E., & Amstutz, L. S. (Eds.). (2008). *Conflict transformation and restorative justice manual: Foundations and skills for mediation and facilitation* (5th ed.). Akron, PA: Office on Justice and Peacebuilding Mennonite Central Committee U.S.

Born, P. (2014). *Deepening community: Finding joy together in chaotic times.* Berrett-Koehler Publishers. Retrieved from https://books.google.ca/books?id=QDEwngEACAAJ

Brown, H. D. (2001). *Teaching by principles: An interactive approach to language pedagogy,* 2nd Ed. White Plains, NY: Longman.

Burns, R. J., & Aspeslagh, R. (2014). *Three decades of peace education around the world: An anthology.* New York: Routledge. Retrieved from https://books.google.ca/books?id=4KymAgAAQBAJ

CAEP Glossary (2010). Downloaded from http://uprm.edu/cms/index.php?a=file&fid=5380

Del Felice, C., Karako, A., & Wisler, A. (Eds.). (2015). *Peace education evaluation: Learning from experience and exploring prospects.* Charlotte, NC: Information Age Publishing.

Dormer, J. E. (2011). *Teaching English in missions: Effectiveness and integrity.* Pasadena, CA: William Carey Library Publishers.

_____. (2012). *Passport to adventure: Explore A.* Colorado Springs, CO: Purposeful Design Publishers.

_____. (2013). *Passport to adventure: Explore B.* Colorado Springs, CO: Purposeful Design Publishers.

_____. (2016). *What school leaders need to know about English learners.* Alexandria, VA: TESOL Press.

_____. (2018). Language Immersion. In J. I. Liontas (Ed.), *TESOL encyclopedia of English Language Teaching* (forthcoming). Hoboken, NJ: Wiley-Blackwell.

Freeman, L. (2007). An overview of dispositions in teacher education. In Diez, M. E. & Raths, J. D. (Eds.), *Dispositions in teacher education* (pp. 3–30). Charlotte, NC: Information Age Publishing.

Freire, P., & Ramos, M. B. (2000). *Pedagogy of the oppressed*. New York, NY: Continuum International Publishing Group.

Gilligan, J. (2001). *Preventing Violence*. London: Thames & Hudson.

Haralambos, M., & Holborn, M. (1991). *Sociology: Themes and perspectives* (3rd ed.). Collins Educational.

Harris, I. M., & Morrison, M. L. (2012). *Peace education* (3rd ed.). Jefferson, NC: McFarland. Retrieved from https://books.google.ca/books?id=NWsrAwAAQBAJ

Hastings, C., & Jacob, L. (Eds.). (2016). *Social justice in English language teaching*. Alexandria, VA: TESOL Press.

Keeves, J. P., & Watanabe, R. (2013). *The international handbook of educational research in the Asia-Pacific region*. Berlin, Germany: Springer Science + Business Media. Retrieved from https://books.google.ca/books?id=BIDvCAAAQBAJ

Kramsch, C. (1998). *Language and culture*. Oxford: Oxford University Press.

Krashen, S. (1981). *Second language acquisition and second language learning*. New York: Pergamon.

Kraybill, R., & Wright, E. (2007). *The little book of cool tools for hot topics: Group tools to facilitate meetings when things are hot*. Brattleboro, VA: Good Books. Retrieved from https://books.google.ca/books?id=hiNrAAAACAAJ

Kuhl, P. (April 3, 2012.) *Babies' Language Skills.* Talk presented at Mind, Brain, and Behavior Annual Distinguished Lecture Series in Harvard University, Cambridge.

Lakey, G. (2010). *Facilitating group learning: Strategies for success with adult learners*. San Francisco, CA: Jossey-Bass. Retrieved from https://books.google.ca/books?id=U9iZT58ls8MC

Lederach, J. P. (2014). *Reconcile: Conflict transformation for ordinary Christians.* Harrisonburg, VA: Herald Press.

Lightbown, P. & Spada, N. M. (2013). *How languages are learned* (4th ed.). Oxford: Oxford University Press.

Lyon, G. E. (2016). Where I'm From. Retrieved from http://www.georgeellalyon.com/where.html

Navarro-Castro, L., & Nario-Galace, J. (2010). *Peace education: A pathway to a culture of peace* (2nd ed.). Quezon City, Philippines: Center for Peace Education, Miriam College.

Norton, B. (2013). *Identity and language learning: Extending the conversation.* Bristol, UK: Multilingual Matters.

_____. (2016). Identity and language learning: Back to the future. *TESOL Quarterly*, 50(2), 475–479. http://doi.org/10.1002/tesq.293

Norton, B., & Toohey, K. (2011). Identity, language learning, and social change. *Language Teaching*, 44(04), 412–446. http://doi.org/10.1017/S0261444811000309

Salomon, G. (2002). The nature of peace education: Not all programs are created equal. In G. Salomon & B. Nevo (Eds.), *Peace education: The concept, principles, and practices around the world.* (pp. 3–14). Mahwah, NJ: Lawrence Erlbaum Associates.

Salomon, G., & Nevo, B. (2002). *Peace education: The concept, principles, and practices around the world.* Mahwah, NJ: Lawrence Erlbaum Associates.

Saunders, H. H. (2012). *Sustained dialogue in conflicts: Transformation and change.* Palgrave Macmillan. Retrieved from https://books.google.ca/books?id=yRleAQAAQBAJ

Schirch, L. (2004). *The little book of strategic peacebuilding.* Intercourse, PA: Good Books. Retrieved from http://books.google.com/books?id=cIuNNAAACAAJ&dq=strategic+peacebuilding&ei=KTbLS9KvLJqsNaDg-KMG&cd=1

_____. (2013). *Conflict assessment and peacebuilding planning: Toward a participatory approach to human security.* Boulder, CO: Kumarian Press.

Search for Common Ground. (2016). Online Field Guide—Design, Monitoring and Evaluation for Peacebuilding. Retrieved from http://dmeforpeace.org/online-field-guide

Snow, D. (2001). *English teaching as Christian mission: An applied theology.* Scottdale, PA: Herald Press.

Tal-Or, N., Boninger, D., & Gleicher, F. (2002). Understanding the conditions and processes necessary for intergroup contact to reduce prejudice. In G. Salomon & B. Nevo (Eds.), *Peace education: The concept, principles, and practices around the world* (pp. 89–107). Mahwah, NJ: Lawrence Erlbaum Associates.

Taylor, F. (2013). *Self and identity in adolescent foreign language learning.* Bristol, UK: Multilingual Matters.

Tuckman, B. W., & Jensen, M. A. (1977). Stages of small group development revisited. *Group and Organization Studies,* 2(4), 419–427. http://doi.org/10.1177/105960117700200404

Wajnryb, R. (1988). The Dictogloss Method of language teaching: A Text–based, communicative approach to grammar. *English Teaching Forum.* 26(3), 35–38.

Woelk, C. (2015). Naming the space: Evaluating language in peace education through reflective practice. In C. Del Felice, A. Karako, & A. Wisler (Eds.), *Peace education evaluation: Learning from experience and exploring prospects* (pp. 53–66). Charlotte, NC: Information Age Publishing.

Yoder, P. B. (1998). *Shalom: The Bible's word for salvation, justice, and peace.* Nappanee, IN: Evangel Publishing House.

About the Authors

Jan Edwards Dormer was born in Indiana, but moved to Brazil at the age of ten, when her parents were called to ministry there. Upon returning to the US at the age of eighteen, Jan received a Bachelor's degree in Elementary Education from Asbury University, and a Master's in TESOL from Ball State University. She then married Rod, a Canadian, and Rod and Jan established their first home in Ontario, where their two daughters were born. The Dormer family then pursued ministry abroad, in Indonesia, Brazil, and later Kenya. Jan earned a doctorate of education in TESOL at the Ontario Institute for Studies in Education, at the University of Toronto. Jan and her husband now live in Pennsylvania, where Jan is associate professor of TESOL at Messiah College, in the Graduate Program in Education. Jan welcomes correspondence with readers and can be reached at jan.dormer@gmail.com.

Cheryl Woelk is a language instructor and a peace educator. She has worked in various cultural settings, including China, South Korea, East Timor, and with newcomer communities and university language programs in the US and Canada. She currently coordinates the *Language for Peace* project, integrating language and peace education curriculum. She grew up in Saskatchewan, Canada. She holds a BA in English, a certificate in TEFL, an MA in Education from Eastern Mennonite University, and a graduate certificate in peacebuilding from EMU's Center for Justice and Peacebuilding. Cheryl lives in Seoul, South Korea with her spouse and son, where she teaches English and consults on a variety of peace education projects. Cheryl welcomes correspondence with readers and can be reached at language4peace@gmail.com.

Teaching English in Missions
by Jan Dormer

English teaching is common in missions today. However, there has been relatively little discussion on what constitutes effectiveness in English ministries. This book aims to foster such discussion. It first addresses issues of concern in English ministries and then suggests criteria for effectiveness, considerations in teacher preparation, and models for the teaching of English in missions.

Available at missionbooks.org

English Language Teaching in Theological Contexts
by Kitty Purgason

Trends in the field of Teaching English to Speakers of Other Languages (TESOL) have led to specialized English and pedagogy for areas such as business, engineering, hospitality, and so on. The time has come to acknowledge English for Bible and Theology.

English Language Teaching in Theological Contexts explores various models for assisting seminary and Bible college students in learning English while also engaging in their theological coursework. It features chapters by specialists from countries including the U.S., Brazil, Ukraine, India, the Philippines, and Korea. Part one of the book presents language teaching challenges and solutions in various places; part two focuses on specific resources to inspire readers to develop their own materials.

Available at missionbooks.org

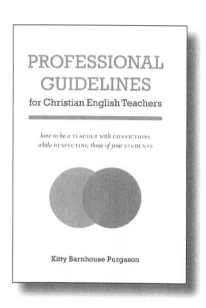

PROFESSIONAL
GUIDELINES
for Christian English Teachers

how to be a TEACHER *with* CONVICTIONS
while RESPECTING *those of your* STUDENTS

Kitty Barnhouse Purgason

Professional Guidelines for Christian English Teachers
by Kitty Purgason

This handbook is for people in the field of English language teaching who are looking for practical ways to be both committed followers of Jesus and ethical TESOL professionals. What do such teachers actually do in the classroom? What materials do they use? How do they relate to their students and colleagues in and outside the classroom? How can they treat students as whole people, with spiritual and religious identities? How can they set a high bar for ethical teaching?

Professional Guidelines for Christian English Teachers has grown out of Kitty Purgason's experience as a Christian seeking to follow the Great Commandment and the Great Commission, as a practitioner with a deep concern for excellence and integrity, and as a teacher trainer with experience in many parts of the world.

Available at missionbooks.org